KU-413-994

Contents

Introduction

Charles Dickens was one of the most popular writers of all time, creating some of the best-known characters in English literature.

He was born in Portsmouth, England in 1812 and moved to London with his family when he was about two years old. The family was very poor, and John Dickens, a clerk with the navy, could not earn enough to support his wife and eight children. Charles, the second oldest, attended school for a short time, but his formal education was cut short. It was his mother who taught him to read and helped him develop a deep love of books. The family's circumstances forced him to leave school at the age of twelve. He found a job in a shoe polish factory and, at about the same time, his father was arrested for debt and sent to prison.

The difficulties the family suffered and the general hopelessness he saw around him as he was growing up shaped Dickens's view of the world and strongly influenced the subject matter, events and characters that featured in his later writing. Determined to break out of a life of insecurity, Dickens started writing for newspapers. He soon made a name for himself as a reporter in London's courts and at the House of Commons.

His first literary success came with the publication, in monthly parts, of what came to be known as *The Pickwick Papers*. By the age of twenty-four he was famous, and remained so until he died. In contrast to his public success, though, Dickens's personal life was not happy. He married Catherine Hogarth in 1836 and they had ten children together. However, as time passed they became increasingly unhappy, and they separated in 1858. Apart from his writing, Dickens found the time and energy to work for various charities, demonstrating the concern for people and social conditions that underlies so much of his writing. Under the strain of many different activities his health suffered and he died suddenly in 1870.

Dickens wrote 20 novels, nearly all of which originally appeared in weekly or monthly parts. By presenting his work in this way in newspapers and magazines, Dickens was able to reach people who would never normally buy full-length books. His wide readership loved the scenes and characters he created that reflected life in mid nineteenth-century London so well. He displayed a great understanding of human nature, a strong sympathy for young people, and a keen eye for people and places. He also wrote a number of works of non-fiction.

Oliver Twist is one of his most famous early books and is based on the adventures of a poor boy whose parents are both dead. It was very influential at the time it was published because it showed the workings of London's criminal world and brought into perspective how the poor were forced to live. The private school system is the main subject of *Nicholas Nickleby*, another early novel. Dickens himself had experienced this world of money-making school owners who mistreated their pupils and taught them nothing. Then, during the 1840s, Dickens wrote five Christmas books. The first of these, *A Christmas Carol*, tells the story of rich and mean Ebenezer Scrooge who, late in life, learns the meaning of Christmas and discovers happiness by helping others less fortunate than himself.

In his later works, including *Hard Times*, *Little Dorrit* and *Our Mutual Friend*, Dickens presents a much darker view of the world. His humour is more pointed, concentrating on the evil side of human experience; in particular, the inhuman social consequences of industry and trade. *Bleak House* shows the unfairness of the contemporary legal system and how lawyers could extend the legal process for their own benefit without any regard for the damage done to the lives of their clients. *David Copperfield* is an exception from this period: a much more light-hearted story and a moving description of a young man's discovery of adult life.

Great Expectations was written while Dickens's own life was hardly ideal: he was in the process of separating from his wife. And yet it is quite brilliant. The book is similar to *David Copperfield* in that it is the story of a boy growing up. It is told by the central character himself, whose name is Pip; Dickens takes the reader right inside the boy's mind, and we live through the events and discoveries of his life with him. Pip has lost his parents and is brought up by his sister and her husband, a blacksmith who takes Pip on as an apprentice and teaches him his trade. The boy's fortunes suddenly change as he is provided with money by a secret benefactor and is able to move to London, receive an education and live as a gentleman. Pip's 'great expectations' do not, however, turn out as he had hoped when one day he makes a surprising discovery.

This is a story of excitement and danger, adventure and murder, but most of all one of self-discovery as Pip painfully rethinks the values on which he has built his life. The reader will enjoy meeting the wide variety of characters – the rich and strange Miss Havisham; honest and kind Joe Gargery; beautiful, heartless Estella, and many others whose influence shapes Pip's life in deep and mysterious ways.

Chapter 1   I Am Told to Steal

My father's family name being Pirrip, and my Christian name
Philip, my infant tongue could make of both names nothing
longer than Pip. So I called myself Pip, and came to be called Pip.
Having lost both my parents in my infancy, I was brought up by
my sister, Mrs Joe Gargery, who married the local blacksmith.

Ours was the marsh country, down by the river, within 20
miles of the sea. My earliest memory is of a cold, wet afternoon
towards evening. At such a time I found out for certain that this
windy place under long grass was the churchyard; and that my
father, mother and five little brothers were dead and buried there;
and that the dark flat empty land beyond the churchyard was the
marshes; and that the low line further down was the river; and
that the distant place from which the wind was rushing was the
sea, and that the small boy growing afraid of it all and beginning
to cry was Pip.

'Hold your noise,' cried a terrible voice, as a man jumped up
from among the graves. 'Keep still, you little devil, or I'll cut your
throat.'

A fearful man, in rough grey clothes, with a great iron on his
leg. A man with no hat, and with broken shoes, and with an old
piece of cloth tied round his head. He moved with difficulty and
was shaking with cold as he seized me by the chin.

'Oh! Don't cut my throat, sir,' I begged him in terror. 'Please,
don't do it, sir.'

'Tell me your name,' said the man. 'Quick!'

'Pip, sir.'

'Once more,' said the man, staring at me. 'Speak out.'

'Pip. Pip, sir.'

'Show me where you live,' said the man. 'Point out the place.'

I pointed to where our village lay, a mile or more from the church.

The man, after looking at me for a moment, turned me upside down and emptied my pockets. There was nothing in them but a piece of bread, which he took and began to eat hungrily.

'You young dog!' said the man, talking as he ate noisily. 'What fat cheeks you've got!'

I believe they were fat, though I was at that time small for my years, and not strong.

He asked me where my father and mother were. When I had pointed out to him the places where they were buried, he asked me who I lived with. I told him I lived with my sister, wife of Joe Gargery, the blacksmith.

On hearing the word 'blacksmith' he looked down at his leg and then at me. He took me by both arms and ordered me to bring him, early the next morning at the old gun placements, a metal file and some food, or he would cut my heart out. I was not to say a word about it all. 'I'm not alone,' he said, 'as you may think I am. There's a young man hidden with me, in comparison with whom I am kind and friendly. That young man hears the words I speak. That young man has a secret way, particular to himself, of getting at a boy, and at his heart. No boy can hide himself from that young man.'

I promised to bring him the file, and what bits of food I could, and wished him goodnight. He moved away towards the low church wall, putting his weight on his one good leg, got over it, and then turned round to look for me. When I saw him turning, I set my face towards home, and made the best use of my legs.

Chapter 2   I Rob Mrs Joe

My sister, Mrs Joe Gargery, was more than 20 years older than I, tall, bony and plain-looking, and had established a great reputation with herself and the neighbours because she had brought me up 'by hand'. Having at that time to find out for myself what the expression meant, and knowing her to have a hard and heavy hand, and to be much in the habit of laying it on her husband, as well as on me, I supposed that Joe Gargery and I were both brought up by hand.

Joe was a fair man, with light brown hair and blue eyes. He was a calm, good-natured, foolish, dear fellow.

When I ran home from the churchyard, Joe's forge, which was joined to our house, was shut up, and Joe was sitting alone in the kitchen.

Joe and I being fellow sufferers, he told me that my sister had been out a dozen times looking for me, and that she had got Tickler (a stick) with her. Soon after that he saw her coming, and advised me to get behind the door, which I did at once.

My sister, throwing the door wide open, and finding something behind it, immediately guessed it was me, and beat me with her stick. She concluded by throwing me at Joe, who, glad to get hold of me on any terms, passed me on into the chimney corner and quickly put himself between her and me.

'Where have you been, you young monkey?' said Mrs Joe, stamping her foot. 'Tell me immediately what you've been doing to wear me away with fear and worry, or I'd have you out of that corner if you were 50 Pips, and he was 500 Gargerys.'

'I have only been to the churchyard,' said I, crying and rubbing myself.

'Churchyard!' repeated my sister. 'If it wasn't for me you'd have been to the churchyard long ago, and stayed there.'

She turned away and started to make the tea; she buttered a

loaf, cut a very thick piece off, which she again cut into two halves, of which Joe got one, and I the other.

Though I was hungry, I dared not eat mine, for I had to have something in reserve for the frightening man on the marshes, and his friend, the still more frightening young man. I took advantage of a moment when Joe was not looking at me, and got my bread and butter down the leg of my trousers.

Joe was shocked to see my bread disappear so suddenly, and thought that I had swallowed it all in one mouthful. My sister also believed this to be the case, and insisted on giving me a generous spoonful of a hateful medicine called "Tar Water", which she poured down my throat.

The guilty knowledge that I was going to rob Mrs Joe and, the constant need to keep one hand on my bread and butter as I sat or walked, almost drove me out of my mind. Happily I managed to slip away, and put it safely in my bedroom.

On hearing big guns fired, I inquired from Joe what it meant, and Joe said, 'Another convict's escaped. There was a convict off last night, escaped from the hulks, and they fired warning of him. And now it appears they are firing warning of another.'

I kept asking so many questions about convicts and hulks that my sister grew impatient with me, and told me that people were put in hulks because they murdered and robbed and lied, and that they always began by asking questions.

As I went upstairs in the dark to my bedroom I kept thinking of her words with terror in my heart. I was clearly on my way to the hulks, for I had begun by asking questions, and I was going to rob Mrs Joe.

I had a troubled night full of fearful dreams, and as soon as the day came I went as quietly as I could to the kitchen, which was full of food for Christmas. I stole some bread, a hard piece of cheese, some sugared fruits, some whisky from a stone bottle, (adding water to replace what I had taken), a bone with very little meat on it, and a beautiful round meat pie, which I thought was not intended for early use, and would not be missed for some time.

Having also taken a file from among Joe's tools in the forge, I ran for the misty marshes.

Chapter 3   The Two Men on the Marshes

It was a freezing cold morning, and very wet. On the marshes the mist was so heavy that gates and fences appeared unexpectedly and seemed to rush towards me.

I was getting on towards the river, but however fast I went, I couldn't warm my feet. I knew my way to the gun placements, but in the confusion of the mist I found myself too far to the right, and had to turn back along the riverside. Suddenly I saw the man sitting in front of me. His back was towards me, and he had his arms folded and was nodding forward, heavy with sleep.

I thought he would be more pleased if I came upon him with his breakfast, in that unexpected manner, so I went forward softly and touched him on the shoulder. He instantly jumped up, and it was not the same man, but another man.

And yet this man was dressed in rough grey clothes, too, and had an iron on his leg, and was shaking with cold, and was everything that the other was, except he had not the same face. He swore at me and hit out wildly but missed me. Then he ran away and disappeared into the mist.

'It's the young man!' I thought, feeling my heart jump as I identified him.

I was soon at the gun placements after that, and there was the right man waiting for me. He was very cold, and his eyes looked awfully hungry. As soon as I emptied my pockets he started forcing the food I had brought into his mouth, pausing only to take some of the whisky. He shook with cold as he swallowed bread, cheese, fruit and meat pie, all at once, staring distrustfully at me and often stopping to listen to any sounds coming through the mists. Suddenly he said: 'You're not a deceiving little devil? You brought no one with you?'

'No, sir. No.'

'Nor did you tell anyone to follow you?'

'No.'

'Well,' said he, 'I believe you. You'd be a young dog indeed, if at your time of life you could help to hunt a pitiful man like me.'

As he sat eating the pie, I told him that I was afraid he would not leave any of it for the young man. He told me with something like a laugh that the young man didn't want any food.

I said that I thought he looked as if he did, and that I had seen him just then, dressed like him and with an iron on his leg, and I pointed to where I had met him. He asked excitedly if he had a mark on his left cheek, and when I replied that he had, he ordered me to show him the way to him and, taking the file from me, he sat down on the wet grass, filing at his iron like a madman. Fearing I had stayed away from home too long, I slipped off and left him working hard at the iron.

Chapter 4   Mr Pumblechook Tastes Tar Water

I fully expected to find a policeman in the kitchen waiting to take me away. But not only was there no policeman, but no discovery had yet been made of the robbery.

Mrs Joe was very busy getting the house ready for Christmas dinner. We were to have a leg of meat and vegetables, and a pair of stuffed chickens. A large pie had been made yesterday morning, and the pudding was already on the boil. Meanwhile, Mrs Joe put clean white curtains up, and uncovered the furniture in the little sitting room across the corridor, which was never uncovered at any other time. Mrs Joe was a very clean housekeeper, but somehow always managed to make her cleanliness more uncomfortable than dirt itself.

Mr Wopsle, the clerk at church, was having dinner with us; and Mr Hubble, the wheel-maker, and Mrs Hubble; and Uncle Pumblechook (Joe's uncle, but Mrs Joe called him *her* uncle), who was a well-to-do corn dealer in the nearest town and had his own carriage. The dinner hour was half past one. When Joe and I got home from church, we found the table laid, and Mrs Joe dressed, and the dinner being prepared, and the front door unlocked for the company to enter by, and everything most perfect. And still not a word of the robbery.

The dinner hour came without bringing with it any relief to my feelings, and the company arrived.

'Mrs Joe,' said Uncle Pumblechook, a large, hard-breathing, middle-aged, slow man, with a mouth like a fish, dull staring eyes and sandy hair standing upright on his head, 'I have brought you, to celebrate the occasion — I have brought you, madam, a bottle of white wine — and I have brought you, madam, a bottle of red wine.'

Every Christmas Day he presented himself with exactly the same words, and carrying the same gift of two bottles. Every Christmas Day, Mrs Joe replied, as she now replied, 'Oh, Uncle Pumblechook! This is kind!' Every Christmas Day, he replied, as he now replied, 'It's no more than you deserve. And now are you all in good spirits, and how's the boy?' meaning me.

We ate on these occasions in the kitchen, and then returned to the sitting room for the nuts and oranges and apples. Among this good company I should have felt myself, even if I hadn't stolen the food, in a false position. Not because I was seated uncomfortably at the corner with the table in my chest and Mr Pumblechook's elbow in my eye, nor because I was not allowed to speak (I didn't want to speak), nor because I was given the bony parts of the chickens and the worst parts of the meat. No, I would not have minded that, if they would only have left me alone. But they wouldn't leave me alone. They seemed to think the opportunity lost, if they failed to point the conversation at me, every now and then, and stick the point into me.

It began the moment we sat down to dinner. Mr Wopsle said a short prayer which ended with the hope that we might be truly grateful. Upon which my sister fixed me with her eye, and said, in a low voice, 'Do you hear that? Be grateful.'

'Especially,' said Mr Pumblechook, 'be grateful, boy, to those who brought you up by hand.'

Joe's position and influence were weaker when there was company than when there was none. But he always aided and comforted me when he could, in some way of his own, and he always did so at dinnertime by giving me gravy, if there was any. There being plenty of gravy today, Joe spooned onto my plate, at this point, about half a pint.

'He was a world of trouble to you, madam,' said Mrs Hubble, sympathizing with my sister.

'Trouble?' repeated my sister. 'Trouble?' and then entered on a fearful catalogue of all the illnesses I had been guilty of, and all the acts of sleeplessness I had committed, and all the high places I had fallen from, and all the low places I had fallen into, and all the injuries I had done myself, and all the times she had wished me in my grave, and I had continually refused to go there.

'Have a little whisky, Uncle,' said my sister.

Oh dear, it had come at last! He would find it was weak, he would say it was weak, and I was lost. I held tight to the leg of the table under the cloth, with both hands, and waited for what I knew would happen.

My sister went for the stone bottle, came back with it, and poured his whisky out; no one else taking any. He took up his glass, looked at it through the light, put it down – extended my misery. All this time Mrs Joe and Joe were clearing the table for the pie and pudding.

I couldn't keep my eyes off him. Still holding tight to the leg of the table with my hands and feet, I saw the miserable creature take up his glass, smile, throw his head back, and drink the whisky all at once. Instantly, the company was seized with unspeakable terror, because of his springing to his feet, turning round several times in a wild coughing dance, and rushing out at the door; he then became visible through the window, violently coughing, making the most terrible faces and appearing to be out of his mind.

I held on tight, while Mrs Joe and Joe ran to him. I didn't know how I had done it, but I had no doubt I had murdered him somehow. In my awful situation, it was a relief when he was brought back, and, surveying the company all round as if they had disagreed with him, sank down into his chair shouting, 'Tar!'

I had filled up the bottle with Tar Water. I knew he would be worse by and by.

'Tar!' cried my sister in amazement. 'Why, how ever could Tar come there?'

Uncle Pumblechook asked for hot gin-and-water. My sister, who had begun to be alarmingly thoughtful, had to employ herself in getting the gin, the hot water and the sugar, and mixing them. For the time at least, I was saved.

By degrees everything became calm again and I was able to eat a little pudding along with everyone else. By the time the course was finished Mr Pumblechook had begun to look a little happier – no doubt helped by the generous amounts of gin-and-water he had drunk.

'You must taste,' said my sister, addressing the guests with her best grace, 'you must taste, to finish with, Uncle Pumblechook's wonderful gift!'

Must they! Let them not hope to taste it!

'You must know,' said my sister, rising, 'it's a pie: a tasty meat pie.'

My sister went out to get it. I heard her steps proceed to the pantry. I saw Mr Pumblechook balance his knife. I felt that I could bear no more, and I must run away. I released the leg of the table, and ran for my life.

But I ran no farther than the front door, for there I ran straight into a party of soldiers with their guns, one of whom held out a pair of handcuffs to me, saying, 'Here you are, come on!'

Chapter 5   The Convicts Are Chased

The arrival of the soldiers caused the dinner party to rise from table in confusion, and caused Mrs Joe, reentering the kitchen empty-handed, to stop short and stare, shouting, 'Goodness me, what's happened to the pie?'

'Excuse me, ladies and gentlemen,' said the sergeant, 'I am on a chase in the name of the King, and I want the blacksmith.' The sergeant then explained that the lock of one of the handcuffs had gone wrong, and as they were wanted for immediate service, he asked the blacksmith to examine them. On being told by Joe that the job would take about two hours, the sergeant asked him to set about it at once, and called on his men to help.

I was extremely frightened. But, beginning to realize that the handcuffs were not for me, and that the arrival of the soldiers had caused my sister to forget about the pie, I pulled myself together a little.

Mr Wopsle asked the sergeant if they were chasing convicts. 'Ay!' returned the sergeant. 'Two. They're pretty well known to be out on the marshes still, and they won't try to get clear of them before dark. Anybody here seen anything of them?'

Everybody except myself said no, with confidence.

Nobody thought of me.

Joe had got his coat off, and went into the forge. One of the soldiers lit the fire, while the rest stood round as the flames turned the coals red. Then Joe began to hammer and we all looked on.

At last, Joe's job was done, and the hammering stopped. As Joe put on his coat, he suggested that some of us should go down with the soldiers and see the result of the hunt. Mr Wopsle said he would go, if Joe would. Mrs Joe, interested in knowing all about it and how it ended, agreed that Joe should go, and allowed me to go with him.

Nobody joined us from the village, for the weather was cold and threatening, with darkness coming on, and the people had good fires indoors and were staying in. A cold rain started to fall as we left the churchyard and struck out on the open marshes, and Joe took me on his back.

The soldiers were moving on in the direction of the old gun placements, and we were moving on a little way behind them, when, all of a sudden, we all stopped. For there had reached us on the wings of the wind and rain, a long shout. It was repeated. There seemed to be two or more shouts raised together. As we came nearer to the shouting, we could hear one voice calling 'Murder!' and another voice, 'Escaped convicts! Runaways! Guard! This way for the runaway convicts!'

Then both voices would seem to be drowned in a struggle, and then would break out again. When they heard this, the soldiers ran in the direction of the voices, and Joe too.

'Here are both men!' shouted the sergeant, struggling towards two men fighting like animals. 'Give up, you two! Come apart!'

Water and mud were flying everywhere, and blows were being struck, when some more men went down to help the sergeant, and dragged out, separately, the convict I had spoken with and the other one. Both were bleeding and shouting and struggling; but of course I knew them both at once.

'Remember!' said my convict, wiping blood from his face with his torn shirt, and shaking hair from his fingers. 'I took him! I give him up to you! Remember that!'

'It's not much to be particular about,' said the sergeant. 'It won't do you much good, my man, being a runaway convict yourself. Handcuffs there!'

The other convict looked in a terrible state.

'Take notice, guard – he tried to murder me,' were his first words.

'Tried to murder him?' said my convict. 'Try, and not do it? I took him, and gave him up; that's what I did. I not only prevented him from getting off the marshes, but I dragged him here – dragged him this far on his way back. He's a gentleman, if you please. Now the hulk has got its gentleman again, through me. Murder him? Not worth my while to murder him when I could do worse and drag him back!'

The other one still cried, 'He tried – he tried – to murder me. Bear – bear witness.'

'Look here!' said my convict to the sergeant. 'Single-handed I got clear of the prison ship; I ran for it and I did it. I could have got clear of these death-cold marshes too – look at my leg: you won't find much iron on it – if I hadn't discovered that he was here. Let him go free? Let him profit by the means I found out? Let him make me look foolish again? Once more? No, no, no. If I had died at the bottom there, I'd have held on tightly to him, so that you would have been sure to find him in my hold.'

'Enough of this dispute,' said the sergeant. 'Light those torches.'

My convict, looking round for the first time, saw me. I had got down from Joe's back when we came up, and had not moved since. I looked at him eagerly when he looked at me, and slightly moved my hands and shook my head. I had been waiting for him to see me, that I might try to assure him that I was not guilty of giving him away. He gave me a look I did not understand, and it all passed in a moment.

The torches having been lit, the sergeant gave the order to march. After an hour or so we came to a rough wooden hut, and a landing place. There was a guard in the hut, who made some kind of report, and some entry in a book, and the younger convict was taken away with his guard, to go on board first.

Suddenly, my convict turned to the sergeant, and – to the amazement of all – said that he had stolen from the blacksmith's house some bits of food, a pie and a little whisky.

The boat had returned, and his guard was ready, so we followed him to the landing place and saw him put into the boat, which was rowed by a crew of convicts like himself.

Somebody in the boat shouted, 'Give way, you!' which was the signal to start rowing. By the light of the torches, we saw the black hulk lying out a little way from the mud of the shore.

Barred and tied by massive, old chains, the prison ship seemed in my young eyes to be in irons like the convicts. We saw the boat go alongside, and we saw him taken up the side and disappear.

Chapter 6   I Am to Go and Play at Miss Havisham's

When I was old enough, I was to start learning to be a blacksmith by working with Joe, and until then I did odd jobs around the forge. Also, if any neighbour happened to want an extra boy to frighten birds, or pick up stones, or do any such job, I was often given the employment.

During this period I attended an evening school kept by Mr

Wopsle's great-aunt. Her method of education was odd, for she usually went to sleep from six to seven every evening, leaving her pupils to improve themselves as best they could by seeing her do it.

Mr Wopsle's great-aunt, besides keeping this Educational Institution, kept – in the same room – a little general shop. She had no idea what stock she had, or what the price of anything in it was; but there was a small notebook kept in a drawer, which served as a catalogue of prices, and by means of it Biddy, who was a distant relation of Mr Wopsle's, arranged all the shop's selling and buying. She, like me, had lost her parents. She too had been brought up by hand.

More by the help of Biddy than by Mr Wopsle's great-aunt, I struggled through my A to Z, getting very worried about every letter. But at last I began to read, write and calculate on the very smallest scale.

◆

Joe had never gone to school in his childhood. One evening, as we were sitting alone by the fire, I wrote him a letter on a slate which I handed to him. Although he could only read his name, he declared me to be very intelligent, and expressed his admiration for my learning. He then told me part of his life story. His father had been a heavy drinker, and he had often struck Joe and his mother, who ran away from him several times and had to work to earn their bread, but he always brought them back. Joe had to work as blacksmith in place of his lazy father, and kept his father until he died, and then his mother died soon after.

Joe then met my sister and asked her hand in marriage, and begged her to bring me with her, saying that there was room for me at the forge.

'So you see, Pip,' Joe said ending his story, 'here we are! Now, when you help me in my learning, Pip, (and I tell you now I am awfully dull), Mrs Joe mustn't see too much of what we're doing. It must be done without her knowing. For your sister is given to government, and she wouldn't like to have clever people in the house, and in particular would not like my being clever, for fear I might rise.'

I was going to ask him, 'Why–' when Joe stopped me.

'Stay a bit. I know what you are going to say. You want to know why I don't rise. Well, your sister's got a good mind and I haven't. And besides, Pip – I see so much in her of my poor mother, a woman slaving and breaking her honest heart and never getting any peace in her life, that I'm afraid of not doing what's right by a woman, and I'd much rather be a little uncomfortable myself. I wish it was only me that got put out, Pip; I wish there were no Tickler for you, old chap; I wish I could take it all on myself; but this is how the matter stands, Pip, and I hope you'll forgive my faults.'

Young as I was, I believe that a new admiration of Joe started that night.

Mrs Joe made occasional trips with Uncle Pumblechook on market days, to assist him in buying such household goods as required a woman's judgment. This was market day, and Mrs Joe was out on one of these trips.

Soon they arrived.

'Now,' said Mrs Joe, unwrapping herself quickly and with excitement, and throwing her hat back on her shoulders, where it hung by the strings. 'If this boy isn't grateful this night, he never will be!'

I looked as grateful as any boy possibly could, who was completely uninformed why he should be so.

'It's only to be hoped,' said my sister, 'that he won't be spoilt. But I have my fears.'

'She is not likely to spoil him,' said Mr Pumblechook. 'She knows better.'

She? I looked at Joe, making the motion with my lips and eyes, 'She?' Joe looked at me, making the motion with *his* lips and eyes.

'Well?' said my sister, in her ill-tempered way. 'What are you staring at? Is the house on fire?'

'Some individual,' Joe said politely, 'referred to-she.'

'And she is a she, I suppose?' said my sister. 'Unless you call Miss Havisham a he. And I doubt if even you'll go so far as that.'

'Miss Havisham up town?' said Joe.

'Is there any Miss Havisham down town?' returned my sister. 'She wants this boy to go and play there. And of course he's going. And he had better play there,' said my sister, shaking her head at me, 'or I'll work him.'

I had heard of Miss Havisham up town – everybody for miles round had heard of Miss Havisham up town – as an extremely rich and strict lady who lived alone in a large dark house.

'Well, to be sure!' said Joe, amazed. 'I wonder how she came to know Pip!'

'Fool!' cried my sister. 'Who said she knew him?'

'Some individual,' Joe again politely continued, 'said that she wanted him to go and play there.'

'And couldn't she ask Uncle Pumblechook if he knew of a boy to go and play there? Isn't it just possible that Uncle Pumblechook may be a tenant of hers, and that he may sometimes go there to pay his rent? And couldn't Uncle Pumblechook, being always kind and thoughtful for us, then mention this boy that I have for ever been a willing slave to?'

'Good again!' cried Uncle Pumblechook. 'Well put! Prettily pointed! Good indeed! Now, Joseph, you know the situation.'

'No Joseph,' said my sister, 'you do not know that Uncle Pumblechook, knowing that this boy's fortune may be made by his going to Miss Havisham's, has offered to take him into town tonight, in his own carriage, and to keep him tonight, and to take him with his own hands to Miss Havisham's tomorrow morning.'

With that, she suddenly seized me, and my head was put under the water tap, and I was soaped, and rubbed until I really was quite beside myself.

I was then put into a clean shirt with a collar and was dressed in my tightest suit, and delivered over to Mr Pumblechook, who started the speech that I knew he had been dying to make all along:

'Boy, be for ever grateful to all friends, but especially to those who brought you up by hand!'

'Goodbye, Joe!' I said.

'God keep you, Pip, old chap!'

I had never parted from him before, and what with my feelings and the soap, I could at first see no stars from the carriage. But they shone out one by one as we moved off, without throwing any light on the question of why on earth I was going to play at Miss Havisham's, and what on earth I was expected to play at.

Chapter 7   I Visit Miss Havisham and Meet Estella

Mr Pumblechook and I breakfasted at eight o'clock in the sitting room at the back of his shop, and at ten we started for Miss Havisham's house, which we reached within a quarter of an hour. It was of old brick, and unwelcoming, and had a great many iron bars to it. Some of the windows had been walled up; of those that remained, all the lower ones were barred. There was a courtyard in front with a big iron gate; so we had to wait, after ringing the bell, until someone came along to open it. While we waited at the gate, I looked in and saw that at the side of the house there was a large brewery.

A window was raised, and a clear voice demanded, 'What

name?' To which my protector replied 'Pumblechook.' The voice returned, 'Quite right,' and the window was shut again, and a young lady came across the courtyard, with keys in her hand.

'This,' said Mr Pumblechook, 'is Pip.'

'This is Pip, is it?' returned the young lady, who was very pretty and seemed very proud. 'Come in, Pip.'

Mr Pumblechook was coming in also, when she stopped him with the gate.

'Oh!' she said. 'Did you wish to see Miss Havisham?'

'If Miss Havisham wished to see me,' returned Mr Pumblechook.

'Ah!' said the girl; 'but you see she doesn't.'

She said it so finally that Mr Pumblechook could not protest. But he eyed me severely — as if I had done something to him — and departed with the words, 'Boy! Let your behaviour be a credit to those who brought you up by hand.'

The young lady locked the gate, and we went across the courtyard, covered in stones but with grass growing between them. The brewery building stood open, and all was empty and disused.

She saw me looking at it, and she said, 'You could drink without hurt all the strong beer that's made there, boy.'

'I should think I could, miss,' said I shyly.

'Better not try to make beer there now, or it would turn out sour, boy; don't you think so?'

'It looks like it, miss.'

'Not that anybody means to try,' she added, 'for that's all done with, and the place will stand as empty as it is, till it falls. As to strong beer, there is enough of it already to drown the Manor House.'

'Is that the name of this house, miss?'

'One of its names, boy.'

'It has more than one, then, miss?'

'One more. Its other name was Satis, which is Greek or Latin for enough.'

'Enough House!' said I. 'That's a strange name, miss.'

'Yes', she replied; 'but it meant more than it said. It meant, when it was given, that whoever had this house could want nothing else. They must have been easily satisfied in those days, I should think. But don't stand there, boy.'

Though she called me 'boy' so often and so carelessly, she was of about my own age. She seemed much older than I, of course, being a girl, and beautiful and self-possessed; and she was as dismissive of me as if she were one-and-twenty and a queen.

We went into the house by a side door, and the first thing I noticed was that the passages were all dark, and that she had left a candle burning there. She took it up and went through more passages and up some stairs, and still it was all dark, and only the candle lit our way.

At last we came to the door of a room, and she said, 'Go in.' She walked away and took the candle with her.

This was very uncomfortable, and I was half afraid. However, I knocked at the door, and was told from within to enter. I entered, and found myself in quite a large room, well-lit with candles. No daylight was to be seen in it. There was a fine lady's dressing table, and in an armchair, with an elbow resting on the table and her head leaning on that hand, sat the strangest lady I have ever seen, or shall ever see.

She was dressed in rich materials – all of white. Her shoes were white. And she had a long white veil hanging from her hair, and she had wedding flowers in her hair, but her hair was white. Some bright jewels shone on her neck and on her hands, and some other jewels lay beside her on the table. She had not quite finished dressing, for she had only one shoe on – the other was on the table near her hand – and her watch and chain were not put on.

Everything within my view which ought to be white had been white long ago, and was now faded and yellow. The old woman within the wedding dress had faded like the dress, and had no brightness left except in her sunken eyes.

She looked at me. I would have cried out, if I could.

'Who is it?' she said.

'Pip, madam.'

'Pip?'

'Mr Pumblechook's boy, madam. Come – to play.'

'Come nearer; let me look at you. Come close.'

It was when I stood before her, avoiding her eyes, that I took note of the surrounding objects in detail, and saw that her watch had stopped at twenty minutes to nine, and that a clock in the room had stopped at twenty minutes to nine.

'Look at me,' said Miss Havisham. 'You are not afraid of a woman who has never seen the sun since you were born?' I answered, 'No', but that was a lie.

'Do you know what I touch here?' she said, laying her hands, one upon the other, on her left side.

'Yes, madam.'

'What do I touch?'

'Your heart.'

'Broken!'

She spoke the word with an eager look, and with strong emphasis, and with a strange smile.

'I am tired,' said Miss Havisham. 'I want something to amuse me, and I have done with men and women. Play. I have a sick fancy that I want to see some play. There, there!' with an impatient movement of her fingers. 'Play, play, play!'

I stood looking at Miss Havisham in what I suppose she took for a rude manner.

'Are you rude, boy?' she said.

'No, madam, I am very sorry for you, and very sorry I can't

play just now. If you complain of me I shall get into trouble with my sister, so I would do it if I could, but it's so new here, and so strange, and so fine and sad–'

'So new to him,' she whispered, 'so old to me; so strange to him, so familiar to me; so sad to both of us! Call Estella. Call Estella, at the door.'

I did so, and when she came, Miss Havisham signalled her to come close, and took up a jewel from the table, and tried its effect upon her fair young chest and against her pretty brown hair.

'Your own, one day, my dear, and you will use it well. Let me see you play cards with this boy.'

'With this boy! Why, he is a common labouring-boy!'

I thought I heard Miss Havisham answer – only it seemed so unlikely – 'Well? You can break his heart.'

'What do you play, boy?' Estella asked me with the greatest contempt.

'Nothing but Beggar My Neighbour, miss.'

'Beggar him,' said Miss Havisham to Estella. So we sat down to cards.

As Estella dealt the cards, I glanced at the dressing table again, and saw that the shoe on it, once white, now yellow, had never been worn.

'What rough hands he has, this boy! And what thick boots!' said Estella with contempt before our first game was over.

I had never thought of being ashamed of my hands before; but I began to consider them rather a bad pair. Her contempt was so strong that it became infectious and I caught it.

She won the game, and I dealt. I misdealt, as was only natural when I knew she was lying in wait for me to do wrong, and she called me a stupid labouring-boy.

'You say nothing of her,' remarked Miss Havisham to me, as she looked on. 'She says many hard things of you, but you say nothing of her. What do you think of her?'

'I don't like to say,' I replied.

'Tell me in my ear,' said Miss Havisham, bending down.

'I think she is very proud,' I replied in a whisper.

'Anything else?'

'I think she is very insulting.'

'Anything else?'

'I think I should like to go home.'

'And never see her again, though she is so pretty?'

'I am not sure that I shouldn't like to see her again, but I should like to go home now.'

'You shall go soon,' said Miss Havisham. 'Play the game out.'

I played the game to an end with Estella, and she beat me. She threw the cards down on the table when she had won them all, as if she hated them for having been won from me.

'When shall I have you here again?' said Miss Havisham. 'Let me think. Come again after six days. Estella, take him down. Let him have something to eat. Go, Pip.'

Estella showed me the way down with a candle, and when she opened the side entrance, the rush of the daylight quite confused me.

'You are to wait here, you boy,' said Estella; and disappeared and closed the door.

Being alone in the courtyard I looked at my rough hands and my thick boots. They had never troubled me before, but they troubled me now. I began to wish that Joe had been rather better brought up, and then I should have been so too.

She came back, with some bread and meat and a little glass of beer. She put the glass down on the ground, and gave me the bread and meat without looking at me, as if I were a dog who had done something wrong. I felt so small that tears came into my eyes. She looked at me with a quick smile at having made me cry, then she left me.

When she was gone, I looked around me for a place to hide

my face in; and got behind one of the gates of the brewery and cried. At last I smoothed my face with my jacket, and came from behind the gate. The bread and meat were acceptable, and the beer was warming.

Soon she approached with the keys to let me out. She opened the gate, and stood holding it. I was passing out without looking at her, when she touched me.

'Why don't you cry?'

'Because I don't want to.'

'You do,' said she. 'You have been crying till you are half blind, and you are near crying again now.'

She laughed, pushed me out, and locked the gate behind me.

I walked home very unhappily, thinking about all I had seen, and deeply conscious that I was a common labouring-boy.

Chapter 8   I Try to Be Uncommon

When I reached home, my sister was very interested in knowing all about Miss Havisham, and asked a number of questions. And I soon found myself getting heavily pushed in the back and having my face shoved against the kitchen wall, because I did not answer those questions at sufficient length.

The worst of it was that that nasty old Pumblechook came over in his carriage at teatime, to have the details revealed to him.

'What is Miss Havisham like?' asked Mr Pumblechook.

'Very tall and dark,' I told him.

'Is she, Uncle?' asked my sister. Mr Pumblechook moved his head in agreement; from which I knew at once that he had never seen Miss Havisham, for she was nothing of the kind.

'What was she doing, when you went in today?' asked Mr Pumblechook.

'She was sitting,' I answered, 'in a black carriage.'

Mr Pumblechook and Mrs Joe stared at one another and both repeated, 'In a black carriage?'

'Yes,' said I. 'And Miss Estella handed her in cake and wine at the carriage window, on a gold plate.'

'Was anybody else there?' asked Mr Pumblechook.

'Four dogs,' said I.

'Large or small?'

'Massive,' said I. 'And they fought for slices of beef out of a silver basket.'

Mr Pumblechook and Mrs Joe stared at one another again, in complete amazement. 'Where was this carriage?' asked my sister.

'In Miss Havisham's room.' They stared again. 'But there weren't any horses to it.'

'What did you play at, boy?' asked Pumblechook.

'We played with flags. Estella waved a blue flag, and I waved a red one, and Miss Havisham waved one with little gold stars. And then we all waved our swords and cheered.'

'Swords!' repeated my sister. 'Where did you get swords from?'

'Out of a cupboard,' said I. 'And I saw guns in it – and sweets – and tablets. And there was no daylight in the room, but it was all lit up with candles.'

They stared at each other again, and were so much occupied in discussing these wonders that I escaped. The subject still held them when Joe came in from his work to have a cup of tea, and my sister told him about my pretended experiences.

Now, when I saw Joe open his blue eyes and roll them in helpless amazement, I was sorry I had told so many lies. After Mr Pumblechook had driven off I stole into the forge to Joe and said to him, 'Joe, you remember all that about Miss Havisham?'

'Remember?' said Joe. 'I believe you! Wonderful!'

'It's a terrible thing, Joe; it's lies. All lies.'

And then I told him that I felt very unhappy, and that I hadn't been able to explain myself to Mrs Joe and Pumblechook, and that there had been a beautiful young lady at Miss Havisham's who was terribly proud, and that she had said I was common, and that the lies had come of it somehow.

After some reflection Joe said, 'There's one thing you may be sure of; that lies are lies. Don't you tell any more of them, Pip. And as to being common, you can't get to be uncommon through lying.'

When I got up to my little room and lay down, I thought of this, but I also thought how common Estella and Miss Havisham would consider Joe, a mere blacksmith: how thick his boots, and how rough his hands.

Chapter 9   I Fight with a Pale Young Gentleman

At the appointed time I returned to Miss Havisham's, and my ring at the gate brought Estella. She led me into the dark passage where her candle stood, and then she took up her candle and said, 'You are to come this way today.' She took me to quite another part of the house.

As we were going along the dark passage, Estella stopped all of a sudden and, turning round, said, with her face quite close to mine:

'Well?'

'Well, miss?' I answered, almost falling over her and stopping myself.

She stood looking at me, and, of course, I stood looking at her.

'Am I pretty?'

'Yes; I think you are very pretty.'

'Am I insulting?'

'Not so much so as you were last time,' said I.

'Not so much so?'

'No.'

Her eyes flashed with anger when she asked the last question, and she hit my face with such force as she had, when I answered it.

'Now?' said she. 'You common little animal, what do you think of me now?'

'I shall not tell you.'

'Because you are going to tell upstairs. Is that it?'

'No,' said I. 'That's not it.'

'Why don't you cry again, you poor little baby?'

'Because I'll never cry for you again,' said I. Which was a lie; for I was crying inside for her then, and I know the pain she cost me afterwards.

We went upstairs after this, to Miss Havisham's room. Estella left me standing near the door, and I stood there until Miss Havisham cast her eyes upon me from the dressing table.

'So!' she said, without being surprised; 'the days have worn away, have they?'

'Yes, madam, today is . . .'

'There, there, there!' with the impatient movement of her fingers. 'I don't want to know. Are you ready to play?'

I answered in some confusion, 'I don't think I am, madam.'

'Not at cards again?' she demanded, with a searching look.

'Yes, madam; I could do that, if I was wanted.'

'Since this house makes you old and serious, boy,' said Miss Havisham impatiently, 'and you are unwilling to play, are you willing to work?'

I said I was quite willing.

'Then go into that opposite room, and wait there till I come.'

I did so, and found that from this room, too, the daylight was quite shut out, and the candles gave only a faint light.

Everything in the room was covered with dust, and dropping to pieces. There was a long table with a tablecloth spread on it, as if a great meal had been in preparation when the house and the clocks all stopped together. In the centre of the table I saw what appeared to be a great pile of cobwebs. I heard the mice too, behind the panels, while big, black insects moved about the fireplace.

While I was watching these things from a distance, Miss Havisham laid a hand on my shoulder. In her other hand she had a stick on which she leaned.

'This', said she, pointing to the long table with her stick, 'is where I will be laid when I am dead. They shall come and look at me here.'

Then, pointing at the cobwebs she said, 'What do you think that is?'

'I can't guess what it is, madam.'

'It's a great cake. A wedding cake. Mine!' She looked all round the room and then said, leaning on my shoulder, 'Come, come, come! Walk me! Walk me!'

I made out from this that the work I had to do was to walk Miss Havisham round and round the room. So I started at once, and she leaned on my shoulder and we went away at a great pace.

After a while she said, 'Call Estella!' So I went out on the landing and called Estella, who came, accompanied by four of Miss Havisham's distant relations, three ladies and a gentleman, each of whom tried to be more polite and to show more love and concern than the others to Miss Havisham.

But they did not deceive her. She knew that all their expressions of affection were false, and that they only came after her money, which they hoped to be left at her death. In return she made fun of them and loaded them with insults to which they dared not respond. All this while she never for one moment paused in her rapid pacing round and round the room.

Then she ordered them to go. While Estella was away lighting them down the stairs, Miss Havisham said to me: 'This is my birthday, Pip. I don't allow those who were here just now, or anyone, to speak of it. They come here on the day, but they dare not refer to it.'

Soon Estella returned and Miss Havisham ordered us to play cards, so we returned to her room, and played as before. Miss Havisham watched us all the time, directed my attention to Estella's beauty, and made me notice it the more by trying her jewels on Estella's chest and hair. When we had played some half-dozen games, a day was appointed for my return, and I was taken down into the yard to be fed in the former dog-like manner. There, too, I was again left to wander about as I liked.

I happened to look in at a window, and found myself, to my great surprise, exchanging looks with a pale young gentleman with light hair.

He quickly disappeared, and then reappeared beside me.

'Hello, young fellow!' said he.

'Hello!' I said.

'Who let you in?' said he.

'Miss Estella.'

'Who gave you permission to wander about?'

'Miss Estella.'

'Come and fight,' said the pale young gentleman.

What could I do but follow him? His manner was so final, and I was so surprised, that I followed where he led, as if I were under a spell.

'Stop a minute, though,' he said. 'I ought to give you a reason for fighting, too. Here it is!' In a most annoying manner he instantly threw one of his legs up behind him, pulled my hair, put his head down and hit me with it hard in the stomach.

I hit out at him, and was going to hit out again when he began dancing backwards and forwards and said, 'Come to the ground.' I followed him to the end of the garden. Then he pulled off not only his jacket, but his shirt too.

Although he did not look very healthy, these awful

preparations quite frightened me. But, to my surprise, as soon as I hit him he fell down on his back, and lay looking up at me with his nose bleeding.

But he was on his feet immediately and, after wiping himself, began fighting again. The second greatest surprise I have ever had in my life was seeing him on his back again, looking up at me out of a black eye.

He seemed so brave that although I had not suggested the fight, I felt little satisfaction in my victory. I got dressed, and said 'Can I help you?' and he said, 'No thank you,' and I said, 'Good afternoon,' and he said, 'Same to you.'

When I got back into the courtyard, I found Estella waiting with the keys. There was a bright red shine to her face, as if something had happened to please her.

'Come here!' she said to me. 'You may kiss me if you like.'

I kissed her cheek as she turned it to me. But I felt that the kiss was given to the rough common boy as a piece of money might have been, and that it was worth nothing.

Chapter 10   Joe at Miss Havisham's

My mind grew very anxious on the subject of the pale young gentleman. The more I thought of the fight and recalled the pale young gentleman on his back, the more certain it appeared that something would be done. For some days I even kept close at home and looked out at the kitchen door with the greatest care before going outside for fear that a policeman should be looking for me. When the day came round for my return to the scene of the fight, my fears reached their height. But I had to go to Miss Havisham's and, after all, nothing was said about our fight, and no pale young gentleman was to be seen.

Outside Miss Havisham's room I saw a chair on wheels. And

that day I started on a regular occupation of pushing Miss Havisham in this chair (when she was tired of walking with her hand on my shoulder) round and round her room, and across the landing, and round the other room.

As we began to be more used to one another, Miss Havisham talked more to me, and asked me what I had learnt and what I was going to be. I told her I was going to be a blacksmith like Joe; and I spoke about knowing nothing and wanting to know everything, in the hope that she might offer some help towards that end. But she did not. Neither did she ever give me any money or anything but my daily dinner.

Estella was always around, and always let me in and out, but never told me I might kiss her again. Sometimes she would coldly put up with me; sometimes she would be quite familiar with me; sometimes she would tell me that she hated me. Miss Havisham would often ask me in a whisper, or when we were alone, 'Does she grow prettier and prettier, Pip?' And when I said 'Yes', she would seem to enjoy it. Sometimes, when Estella's moods were so many and so opposed to one another that I had no idea what to say or do, Miss Havisham would hold her lovingly, whispering in her ear, 'Break their hearts, my pride and hope, break their hearts and have no pity!'

Meanwhile, councils went on in the kitchen at home, between my sister and that ass, Pumblechook. The man would drag me up from my chair (usually by the collar) where I was quiet in a corner, and, putting me in front of the fire as if I were going to be cooked, would begin by saying, 'Now, madam, here is this boy! Here is this boy whom you brought up by hand. Hold up your head, boy, and be forever grateful to them that did so.' And then he and my sister would make such nonsensical guesses about Miss Havisham, and about what she would do with me and for me, that I used to want to burst into tears, fly at Pumblechook and strike him repeatedly.

Joe took no part in these discussions, but my sister saw that he was not favourable to my being taken away from the forge, and she got angry with him and with me.

We went on in this way for a long time. One day Miss Havisham said to me, 'You are growing tall, Pip!'

She said no more about it at that time, but the next time I went to see her, she said:

'Tell me once more the name of that blacksmith of yours.'

'Joe Gargery, madam.'

'He is the master that you are to be apprenticed to?'

'Yes, Miss Havisham.'

'You'd better be apprenticed at once. Would Gargery come here with you, and bring the necessary papers?'

I said I had no doubt he would take it as an honour to be asked.

'Then let him come soon, and come along with you.'

On the next day but one, Joe dressed himself in his Sunday clothes to accompany me to Miss Havisham's. My sister declared her intention of going to town with us, and being left at Uncle Pumblechook's and called for 'when we had done with our fine ladies'.

The forge was shut up for the day, and we walked to town, and Joe and I went straight to Miss Havisham's house.

Estella opened the gate, and the moment she appeared, Joe took his hat off and stood holding it in his hands.

Estella told me we were both to go in, so I took Joe by the arm and led him to Miss Havisham. She was seated at her dressing table, and looked round at us immediately.

'Oh!' said she to Joe. 'You are the husband of the sister of this boy? And you have brought up this boy, with the intention of taking him to train as a blacksmith, is that so, Mr Gargery?'

Throughout the interview, Joe addressed me instead of Miss Havisham; and now he said:

'You know, Pip, that you and I are always friends, and we look forward to your helping me at the forge. But, Pip, if you have any objections to the business, please say so, and they will be attended to.'

'Has the boy,' said Miss Havisham, 'ever made any objection? Does he like the trade?'

Joe said, 'You know, Pip, that it was always the great wish of your heart.'

It was quite impossible to make him realize that he ought to speak to Miss Havisham. The more I made faces to him to do it, the more he insisted on addressing me, evidently thinking it would not be polite to address her.

'Have you brought the papers with you?' asked Miss Havisham.

'Well, Pip,' said Joe, as if that were a little unreasonable, 'you know that you saw me put them into my hat, and so you must know that they are here.' And then he took them out of his hat and gave them, not to Miss Havisham, but to me. I am afraid I was ashamed of the dear good fellow when I saw that Estella stood at the back of Miss Havisham's chair, and that her eyes showed contempt. I took the papers from him and gave them to Miss Havisham.

Miss Havisham read them, and then said to Joe: 'You did not expect any fee for teaching the boy your trade?'

'Joe!' I said, for he made no reply at all. 'Why don't you answer?'

'Pip,' he said, 'that was a question not requiring any answer between you and me, and to which you know very well that the answer is no.'

Miss Havisham took up a little bag from the table beside her.

'Pip has earned some money here,' she said, 'and here it is. There are twenty-five pounds in this bag. Give it to your master, Pip.'

As if he were absolutely out of his mind with wonder at her strange figure and the strange room, Joe, even now, would only speak to me.

'This is very kind of you, Pip,' he said, 'and it is very welcome, although I would never have asked for it.'

'Goodbye, Pip!' said Miss Havisham. 'Let them out, Estella.'

'Am I to come again, Miss Havisham?' I asked.

'No. Gargery is your master now. Gargery! One word!'

Thus calling him back as I went out of the room, I heard her say to Joe: 'The boy has been a good boy here, and that is his reward. Of course, as an honest man, you will expect no other and no more.'

How Joe got out of the room, I have never been able to determine; but I know that when he did get out he was steadily proceeding upstairs instead of coming down, until I went after him and took hold of him. In another minute we were outside the gate, and it was locked, and Estella was gone.

'Well!' cried my sister when we returned to Uncle Pumblechook's. 'What did she give the boy?' Joe asked her and Pumblechook to guess. They considered twenty pounds would be a good reward, but Joe said, happily handing the bag to my sister, 'It's twenty-five pounds.'

'Twenty-five pounds, madam,' said Pumblechook, rising to shake hands with her; 'and it's no more than you deserve, and I wish you joy of the money.' Then, taking me by the arm, he said, 'Now you see, Joseph and wife, I am one of them that always go right through with what they've begun. The contract must be signed, at once. That's my way. Signed at once.'

We at once went over to the town hall to sign the agreement before the magistrate. My papers were signed, and my period of training with Joe began.

When we returned to Pumblechook's, my sister became so excited by the twenty-five pounds that she insisted on our having a dinner at the Blue Boar, to which the Hubbles and Mr Wopsle were invited.

I passed a rather sad day. They wouldn't let me go to sleep, but whenever they saw me dropping off, they woke me up and told me to enjoy myself.

Finally we returned home, and when I got into my little bedroom I was truly unhappy and had a strong belief that I would never like Joe's trade. I had liked it once, but once was not now.

I felt quite low on my first working day, but I am glad to say that I never said a word to Joe about it. It is almost the only thing I am glad to know of myself in that connection.

What I wanted, who can say? How can I say, when I never knew? What I hated the thought of was that in some unlucky hour I, being at my dirtiest and commonest, should lift up my eyes and see Estella looking in at one of the windows of the forge. My biggest fear was that she would, sooner or later, find me, with a black face and hands, doing the worst part of my work, and would laugh at me and hold me in contempt.

Chapter 11   Old Orlick

Joe kept a workman at weekly wages, whose name was Orlick. He was a broad-shouldered, dark fellow of great strength. He had no liking for me, and when I became Joe's apprentice he liked me still less, thinking that I would replace him.

Wishing to pay a visit to Miss Havisham and Estella, I had asked Joe to give me a half-holiday. I was reminding him of this at the forge when Orlick said:

'Now, master! Surely you are not going to favour only one of us. If young Pip has a half-holiday, do as much for Old Orlick.' (He always spoke of himself as Old Orlick.)

'Why, what'll you do with a half-holiday, if you get it?'

'What'll I do with it? What'll he do with it? I'll do as much with it as *him*,' said Orlick.

'As to Pip, he's going up town,' said Joe.

'Well, then, as to Old Orlick, he's going up town,' responded the workman. 'Two can go up town.'

'Don't lose your temper,' said Joe.

'I shall if I like,' replied Orlick. 'Now, master! Come. No favouring in this shop. Be a man!'

'Well,' said Joe, 'as in general you stick to your work as well as most men, let it be a half-holiday for all.'

My sister had been standing silent in the yard, within hearing, and she instantly looked in at one of the windows.

'How like you, you fool!' said she to Joe, 'giving holidays to lazy people like that. You are a rich man, upon my life, to waste wages in that way. I wish *I* was his master!'

'You'd be everybody's master, if you could,' said Orlick.

'Leave her alone,' said Joe.

'I'd be a match for all fools like you,' returned my sister, beginning to work herself into a fearful temper.

'You're a bad woman, Mother Gargery,' shouted Orlick.

'Leave her alone, will you?' said Joe.

'What did you say?' cried my sister, beginning to shout wildly. 'What did you say? What did that fellow Orlick say to me, Pip? What did he call me, with my husband standing by? Oh! Oh! Oh! What was the name he gave me before the creature who swore to defend me? Oh! Hold me! Oh!'

Being now in a mad temper, she rushed at the door, which I had fortunately locked.

What could the unfortunate Joe do now but stand up to his workman and ask him what he meant by causing trouble between himself and Mrs Joe; and further, whether he was man enough to fight. And so they went at one another, these two huge men. But, if any man in that neighbourhood could stand up long against Joe, I never saw that man. Orlick, as if he had been of no more account than the pale young gentleman, was very soon among the coal dust, and in no hurry to come out of it. Then Joe unlocked the door and picked up my sister, who had fallen senseless, and carried her into the house and laid her down.

I went upstairs to dress for my holiday, and when I came down again, I found Joe and Orlick sharing a pot of beer in a friendly manner.

When I reached the town to pay my visit I passed the gate of Miss Havisham's house many times before I could make up my mind to ring the bell.

Inside the house I found everything the same, except that Miss Havisham was alone. 'Well?' said she. 'I hope you want nothing. You'll get nothing.'

'No, indeed, Miss Havisham. I only wanted you to know that I am doing very well in my training, and am always very thankful to you.'

'There, there!' with the old restless fingers. 'Come now and then, come on your birthday. – Ah!' she cried suddenly, turning herself and her chair towards me. 'You are looking round for Estella? Hey?'

I had been looking round, in fact, for Estella, and I managed to say that I hoped she was well.

'Gone,' said Miss Havisham; 'to a good school; far out of reach; prettier than ever; admired by all who see her. Do you feel that you have lost her?'

I was at a loss what to say, but Miss Havisham saved me the trouble of finding an answer by sending me away. When the gate was closed upon me, I felt more dissatisfied than ever with my home and with my trade and with everything.

And that was all I got by going to Miss Havisham's.

I met Mr Wopsle in the town and went with him to see

Uncle Pumblechook. It was a very dark night by the time we set out on the walk home. Beyond the town we walked into a thick wet mist, where we came upon a man who seemed to be waiting for us. It was Orlick. He told us that some convicts must have escaped from the hulks, for he had been hearing guns since dark.

On our way to the village we learnt, at the inn, that our house had been broken into when Joe was out, and that somebody had been attacked and hurt.

We ran home as fast as we could and there we found our kitchen full of people. There was a doctor, and there was Joe, and there was a group of women, all on the floor in the middle of the kitchen. They drew back when they saw me, and I saw my sister lying senseless on the floor where she had been knocked unconscious by a blow to the back of the head by some unknown person.

Nothing had been taken from any part of the house. Neither was there any disorder in the kitchen, except such as she herself had made, in falling and bleeding. But there was one strange piece of evidence on the spot. She had been struck with something heavy, on the head and back. And on the ground beside her was a convict's leg iron which had been filed apart.

I believed the iron to be my convict's iron – the iron I had seen and heard him filing at, on the marshes – but my mind did not accuse him of having put it to its latest use. I suspected Orlick.

It was horrible to think that I had provided the weapon, but I could hardly think otherwise. I suffered unspeakable trouble while I considered whether I should reveal the secret of my childhood, and tell Joe everything, and resolved at last to tell the whole story if I should see any chance of helping in the discovery of the attacker.

The police were in the area for a week or two, and arrested several people who had nothing to do with the attack. But they never took the criminal.

Long after they had gone, my sister lay very ill in bed. Her eyesight, hearing and memory were greatly damaged and her speech was impossible to understand. When at last she came round so far as to be helped downstairs, it was still necessary to keep my slate always by her so that she might indicate in writing what she could not explain in speech.

However, her temper was greatly improved, and she was patient. We were at a loss to find a suitable attendant for her, until Mr Wopsle's great-aunt died, and Biddy came to live with us.

Her presence made a great difference, especially to Joe. She instantly took charge of my sister as though she had studied her from infancy, and Joe became able to enjoy a quieter life and go to the inn now and then for a change that did him good.

Chapter 12   I Tell Biddy My Secrets

Gradually I became conscious of a change in Biddy. Her hair grew bright and neat; her hands were always clean. She was not beautiful – she was common, and could not be like Estella – but she was pleasant and sweet-tempered. She managed our whole domestic life wonderfully and, besides, learnt everything that I learnt and always kept up with me.

One Sunday afternoon we went for a walk together on the marshes. When we came to the riverside and sat down on the bank, with the water at our feet, I decided that it was a good time and place to speak to Biddy.

'Biddy,' said I, after making her promise to keep the secret, 'I want to be a gentleman.'

'Oh, I wouldn't, if I were you!' she returned. 'I don't think it would do; don't you think you are happier as you are?'

'Biddy,' I said impatiently, 'I am not at all happy as I am. My trade is unpleasant, and I never shall be comfortable unless I can lead a very different sort of life from the life I lead now.'

'That's a pity!' said Biddy, shaking her head with a sorrowful air.

Then I told her about Estella, that she thought I was rough and common, that she was more beautiful than anybody ever was, and that I admired her terribly, and wanted to be a gentleman for her sake.

'Do you want to be a gentleman to annoy her or to win her over? Because if it is to annoy her, that might be better done by caring nothing for her words. And if it is to win her over, I should think she was not worth winning over.'

'It may be all quite true,' said I to Biddy, 'but I admire her such a lot.'

Biddy was the wisest of girls, and she tried to reason no more with me. She softly stroked my shoulder, and said, 'I am glad that you have felt you could share your secret with me, Pip.'

'Biddy,' I cried, getting up, putting my arm round her neck, and giving her a kiss, 'I shall always tell you everything.'

'Till you're a gentleman,' said Biddy.

We walked a little further on, and I began to consider whether I was not more naturally situated, after all, in these circumstances, than playing cards by candlelight in the room with the stopped clocks, and being held in contempt by Estella. I asked myself whether I did not surely know that if Estella were beside me at that moment instead of Biddy, she would make me unhappy. I had to admit that I did know it for a certainty, and I said to myself, 'Pip, what a fool you are!'

We talked a good deal as we walked, and all that Biddy said seemed right. Biddy was never insulting; she would have found it upsetting to give me pain; she would far rather have hurt herself than me. How could it be, then, that I did not like her much the better of the two?

'Biddy,' said I, when we were walking home, 'I wish you could put me right.'

'I wish I could!' said Biddy.

'If I could only get myself to fall in love with you – you don't mind my speaking so openly to such an old friend?'

'Oh, dear, not at all!' said Biddy. 'Don't mind me.'

'If I could only get myself to do it, that would be the thing for me.'

'But you never will, you see,' said Biddy.

Near the churchyard we met Orlick.

'Hello!' he said. 'Where are you two going?'

'Where should we be going, but home?'

'Well, then,' he said, 'I'll see you home.'

Biddy was much against his going with us, and said to me in a whisper, 'Don't let him come; I don't like him.' As I did not like him either, I thanked him, but said that we didn't want seeing home. He received that information with a laugh, and then walked slowly behind us at a little distance. I asked Biddy why she did not like him.

'Oh!' she replied. 'Because I – I am afraid he likes me.'

'Did he ever tell you he liked you?' I asked angrily.

'No,' said Biddy, looking over her shoulder, 'he never told me so, but he stares at me whenever he can catch my eye.'

I was very cross indeed about old Orlick's daring to admire her; as cross as if it were an insult to me. I kept an eye on him after that night.

Chapter 13   I Have Great Expectations

It was the fourth year of my training with Joe and it was a Saturday night. We were gathered round the fire at the village inn, listening to Mr Wopsle as he read the newspaper out loud.

It was not till he had finished that I became aware of a strange gentleman leaning over the back of the chair opposite me.

Eventually he came forward and said, looking round at us:

'I have reason to believe there is a blacksmith among you, by the name of Joseph – or Joe – Gargery. Which is the man?'

'Here is the man,' said Joe.

'You have a young man with you,' continued the stranger, 'commonly known as Pip? Is he here?'

'I am here!' I cried. I observed that he had a large head, a dark skin and deep-set eyes.

'I wish to have a private talk with you two,' said he. 'Perhaps we had better go to your house.'

In a wondering silence we three walked home. When we got there we went into the sitting room, and the strange gentleman sat down at the table, drawing the candle to him, and looking over something in his pocketbook. Then he said, 'My name is Jaggers, and I am a lawyer in London. I have unusual business with you. Now, Joseph Gargery, I am here to make you an offer to release this young fellow from his apprenticeship. You would not object to letting him go, at his request and for his good? You would not want anything for doing this?'

'I should not like to stand in Pip's way,' replied Joe; 'and I do not want anything for letting him go.'

'Very well,' said Mr Jaggers. 'Now, what I have to tell you is that Pip has Great Expectations.'

Joe and I looked at one another.

'I am instructed to communicate to him,' said Mr Jaggers, 'that he will come into a large property, and that it is the desire of the present owner of that property that he be immediately removed from this place and be brought up as a gentleman.'

My dream had come true; my wild fancy was becoming reality; Miss Havisham was going to make my fortune.

'Now, Mr Pip,' the lawyer went on, 'I address the rest of what I have to say to you. You are to understand, first, that it is the request of the person from whom I take my instructions that you always bear the name of Pip. Secondly, you are to understand that the name of your benefactor remains a secret, until he chooses to reveal it. You are forbidden to make any inquiry into this matter or any reference to any individual in the communications you may have with me. If you have any objection to these two conditions, now is the time to mention it. Speak out.'

I said with difficulty that I had no objection, and Mr Jaggers went on:

'I should think not! Now, Mr Pip, we come next to mere details of arrangement. I have with me a sum of money sufficient for your education and expenses. You will please consider me your guardian. It is considered that you must be better educated, to suit your changed circumstances.'

I said I had always longed for it.

Mr Jaggers then suggested the name of Mr Matthew Pocket, whom I had heard Miss Havisham mention as one of her relations, to be my teacher, and I expressed my thanks to Mr Jaggers for this choice, and said I would gladly try that gentleman.

'Good. You had better try him in his own house. The way shall be prepared for you, and you can see his son first, who is in London. When will you come to London?'

I said, looking at Joe, who stood looking on, motionless, that I supposed I could come immediately.

'First,' said Mr Jaggers, 'you should have some new clothes to come in. Say a week from today. You'll want some money. Shall I leave you twenty pounds?'

He counted them out on the table and pushed them over to me. Then he gave Joe a long look.

'Well, Joseph Gargery. You look very surprised indeed.'

'I am,' said Joe in a very decided manner.

'It was understood that you wanted nothing for yourself, remember. But what if it was in my instructions to make you a present, as compensation?'

'As compensation for what?' Joe demanded.

'For the loss of his services.'

Joe laid his hand gently upon my shoulder and said, 'Pip is welcome to go free to honour and fortune. If you think that money can be a compensation for the loss of the little child who came to the forge, and with whom I have always been the best of friends . . .' and then he could say no more.

'Now, Joseph Gargery,' said Mr Jaggers, 'I warn you this is your last chance. No half measures with me. If you mean to take a present that I have permission to offer you, speak, and you shall have it. If, on the other hand, you mean to say–' Here, to his great amazement, he was stopped by Joe's suddenly getting ready to fight him.

'Well, Mr Pip,' said the lawyer, 'I think the sooner you leave here – as you are to be a gentleman – the better. Let it be a week from today, and you shall receive my address before then. You can take a coach at the coach office in London, and come straight to me.'

When he had left us, Joe locked the front door and we sat by the kitchen fire, staring at the burning coals, and nothing was said for a long time.

My sister was in her usual chair, Biddy sat sewing on one side of Joe, and I sat on his other side.

At last I said, 'Joe, have you told Biddy?'

'I left it to you, Pip.'

'I would rather you told her, Joe.'

'Pip is a gentleman of fortune then,' said Joe, 'and God keep him in it!'

Biddy dropped her work and looked at me. Joe held his knees and looked at me. I looked at both of them. After a pause, they both held me warmly and said how pleased they were for me; but there was a certain touch of sadness in their words that made me sad.

Biddy tried hard to explain to my sister some idea of what had happened, but her efforts failed completely.

Two days later I put on the best clothes I had, and went into town as early as I could hope to find the shops open. First I visited a clothes shop, where I was measured for a new suit. After that I went to the hatter's and the bootmaker's and to other shops. Then I went to Mr Pumblechook's. He had called at the forge and heard the news, and had prepared a light meal in my honour. He took me with both hands and made much of me, as if we had always been the best of friends.

'To think,' said Mr Pumblechook, after admiring me for some moments, 'that I should have some responsibility for this, is a proud reward.'

I begged Mr Pumblechook to remember that nothing was ever to be said on that point.

Mr Pumblechook helped me to chicken, to the best pieces of tongue, and to wine, and shook hands with me many times. He also made known to me for the first time in my life that he had always said of me, 'That boy is no common boy, and mark me, his fortune will be no common fortune.' At last I took my leave and returned home.

◆

The days passed, and on Friday morning I went again to Mr Pumblechook's to put on my new clothes and pay my visit to Miss Havisham. Sarah Pocket, apparently an occasional companion for Estella, opened the gate for me and took me upstairs. Miss Havisham was taking exercise in the room with the long table, leaning on her stick.

'I start for London tomorrow, Miss Havisham,' I said, 'and I thought you might kindly allow me to take leave of you.'

'This is a happy sight, Pip,' said she, making her stick play round me, as if she, the benefactor who had changed me, were putting the finishing touches to her gift.

'I have come into such good fortune since I saw you last, Miss Havisham,' I said quietly. 'And I am so grateful for it, Miss Havisham!'

'Ay, ay!' said she, looking delightedly at the jealous Sarah Pocket. 'I have seen Mr Jaggers. I have heard about it, Pip. So you go tomorrow?'

'Yes, Miss Havisham.'

'And you are adopted by a rich person?'

'Yes, Miss Havisham.'

'Not named?'

'No, Miss Havisham.'

'And Mr Jaggers is made your guardian?'

'Yes, Miss Havisham.'

'Well!' she went on. 'You have a promising career before you. Be good – deserve it and follow Mr Jaggers's instructions.' She looked at me, and looked at Sarah, and the look on Sarah's face brought a cruel smile to her own. 'Goodbye, Pip! – you will always keep the name of Pip, you know.'

'Yes, Miss Havisham.'

'Goodbye, Pip!'

She stretched out her hand, and I went down on my knee and put it to my lips, and so I left her. I returned to Pumblechook's, took off my new clothes and went back home in my older dress, feeling – to speak the truth – much more comfortable.

And now those six days which were to have run out so slowly had run out fast and were gone, and tomorrow looked me in the face more steadily than I could look at it.

I was to leave our village at five in the morning, and I had told Joe that I wished to walk away all alone. All night there were coaches in my broken sleep, going to wrong places instead of to London, now drawn by dogs, now by cats, now by men – never by horses. Strange failures of journeys occupied me until the day came and the birds were singing. Then I got up and dressed, but could not bring myself to go downstairs, until Biddy called to me that I was late.

It was a hurried breakfast with no taste in it. I kissed my sister and Biddy, and threw my arms around Joe's neck. Then I took up my little bag and walked out.

I walked away at a good pace, thinking it was easier to go than I had supposed it would be. I whistled and made nothing of going. But the village was very peaceful and quiet, and I had been so small and childish there, and all beyond was so unknown and great, that in a moment I broke into tears. It was by the signpost at the end of the village, and I laid my hand upon it, and said, 'Goodbye, my dear, dear friend!'

This is the end of the first stage of Pip's expectations.

Chapter 14   In London with the Pockets

The journey from our town to the capital was a journey of about five hours. When I arrived at Mr Jaggers's office the clerk told me that he was in court, and that he had left word I should wait in his room. He led me to a dark room. After I had waited for a long time Mr Jaggers arrived.

Many people, men and women, who had been waiting for him outside the office, made a rush at him. He addressed himself to two of the men.

'Now, I have nothing to say to *you*,' said Mr Jaggers, pointing his finger at them. 'I want to know no more than I know. As to the result, it could go either way. I told you that from the start. Have you paid Wemmick?'

'Yes, sir,' said both the men together.

'Very well; then you may go. Now, I won't have it!' said Mr

Jaggers, waving his hand at them to put them behind him. 'If you say a word to me, I'll throw up the case.'

'We thought, Mr Jaggers—' one of the men began, pulling off his hat.

'That's what I told you not to do,' said Mr Jaggers. '*You* thought! I think for you; that's enough for you. If I want you, I know where to find you; I don't want you to find me. Now I won't have it. I won't hear a word.'

The two men looked at one another as Mr Jaggers waved them behind him, and fell back and were heard no more.

Having dealt with the other people in the same manner, my guardian took me into his own room, where he told me I was to go to Barnard's Inn, to young Mr Pocket's rooms, where a bed had been sent in for my use. I was to remain with young Mr Pocket until Monday; on Monday I was to go with him to his father's house on a visit, so I might see how I liked it. He handed me my allowance, the cards of certain shopkeepers with whom I was to deal for all kinds of clothes, and such other things I might want. Wemmick, his clerk, was to accompany me to young Mr Pocket's house.

Casting my eyes on Mr Wemmick as we went along, I found him to be a dry man, rather short, with a square wooden face. I judged him to be unmarried, from the worn-out condition of his clothes. He had shining eyes – small, keen, and black – and thin wide lips.

'So you were never in London before?' said Mr Wemmick to me.

'No,' said I, 'is it a very bad place?'

'You may get cheated, robbed and murdered in London,' he said. 'But there are plenty of people anywhere who'll do that for you.'

Eventually we arrived at Barnard's Inn, where Mr Herbert Pocket lived. It was a collection of old run-down houses divided into flats, many of which were to let.

Mr Wemmick led me up a flight of stairs to a flat on the top floor. MR POCKET, JUNIOR was painted on the door, and there was a note on the letterbox on which was written, 'Back soon'. Mr Wemmick wished me good day and left me.

It was not before a long half-hour had passed that I heard Herbert's footsteps on the stairs. He had a paper bag under each arm and a little basket of fruit in one hand, and was out of breath.

'Mr Pip?' said he.

'Mr Pocket?' said I.

'Dear me!' he exclaimed. 'I am extremely sorry; but I knew there was a coach from your part of the country at midday, and I thought you would come by that one.'

After some efforts with the door, it opened at last and we went in. Mr Pocket then said, 'My father thought you would like to spend the Sunday with me rather than with him, and might like to take a walk around London. I am sure I shall be happy to show London to you. Our rooms are not as comfortable as I would like, because I have my own bread to earn. This is your bedroom; the furniture is hired for the occasion, but I hope it is good enough.'

As I stood in front of Mr Pocket, Junior, he gave me a sudden look of surprise and said in amazement:

'I can't believe it – you're the boy I fought with!'

'And you,' said I, 'are the pale young gentleman!'

We stood looking at one another until we both burst out laughing. 'The idea of it being you!' said he.

'The idea of it being *you*!' said I.

'You hadn't come into your good fortune at that time?' said Herbert Pocket.

'No,' said I.

'No,' he agreed: 'I heard it had happened very lately. I was rather on the look-out for good fortune then. Miss Havisham had sent for me, to see if she could take a fancy to me. But she couldn't – at all events, she didn't. If I had been successful, perhaps I should have been engaged to Estella.'

'How did you bear your disappointment?'

'Pooh!' said he, 'I didn't care much for it. She's a quick-tempered girl. She's hard and thinks a lot of herself, and has been brought up by Miss Havisham to make all the male sex suffer.'

'What relation is she to Miss Havisham?'

'None,' said he. 'Only adopted.'

'Why should she want to make all the male sex suffer?'

'Lord, Mr Pip!' said he. 'Don't you know?'

'No,' said I.

'Dear me! It's quite a story, and shall be saved till dinnertime.'

Herbert Pocket had an open and easy way with him that was very attractive. I have never seen anyone who more strongly expressed to me, in every look and tone, a natural inability to do anything secret and mean. There was something wonderfully hopeful about him, and something that at the same time whispered to me he would never be successful or rich.

I told him my story, and laid stress on my being forbidden to inquire who my benefactor was.

At dinnertime he told me Miss Havisham's story. 'Miss Havisham,' he began, 'was a spoilt child. Her mother died when she was a baby; and her father gave her everything she wanted. Mr Havisham was very rich and very proud. So was his daughter. She was not his only child; she had a half-brother. Her father had married again – his cook, I rather think.'

'I thought he was proud.'

'So he was. He married his second wife secretly, and in the course of time she died. When she was dead, he told his daughter what he had done, and then the son became a part of the family, living in the house you went to. As the son grew to be a young man, he became wild and altogether bad. Finally his father cut him off; but he regretted this when he was dying, and left him well off, though not nearly so well off as Miss Havisham. He wasted his money and got very much into debt. Then a man appeared on the scene who appeared to fall in love with Miss Havisham. He pursued her closely, and she loved him deeply. He took advantage of her affection and got great sums of money from her. Her relations were poor and clever, with the exception of my father; he was poor enough, but not jealous of her money. The only independent one among them, he warned her that she was doing too much for this man, and was placing herself too much in his power. She took the first opportunity of angrily ordering my father out of the house, in the presence of this man, and my father has never seen her since. To return to the man and make an end of him. The marriage day was fixed, the wedding guests were invited. The day came, but not the husband-to-be. He wrote a letter–'

'Which she received,' I broke in, 'when she was dressing for her marriage? At twenty minutes to nine?'

'At the hour and minute,' agreed Herbert, 'at which she afterwards stopped all the clocks. When she recovered from a bad illness that she had, she left everything in the house untouched, as you have seen it, and she has never since looked upon the light of day.'

'Is that all the story?' I asked, after thinking about it.

'All I know of it. But I have forgotten one thing. It has been supposed that the man to whom she gave her confidence acted throughout in agreement with her half-brother; that it was a plan between them; and that they shared the money he took from her.'

'I wonder he didn't marry her and get all the property,' said I.

'He may have been married already.'

'What became of the two men?' I asked.

'They fell into deeper shame and dishonour – if there can be deeper – and ruin.'

'Are they alive now?'

'I don't know. You now know all that I know about Miss Havisham.'

I asked Herbert, in the course of conversation, what his occupation was. He told me he was in finance – the insurance of ships. But there was no sign of finance or of ships in the room.

'I shall not rest satisfied,' said he, 'with merely using my money to insure ships. I shall buy some good shares, and also do a little in the mining way. I think I shall trade with the East Indies, for silks, materials and hard woods. It's an interesting trade.'

'Is there a lot of money to be made?' said I.

'A large amount,' said he. 'I think I shall trade, also, with the West Indies, for sugar, tobacco and wine.'

'You will want a good many ships,' said I.

'Indeed,' said he. Quite overcome by the greatness of this business, I asked him where the ships he insured traded at present.

'I haven't even begun insuring yet,' he replied. 'I am busy just looking about me. I am with a firm of accountants.'

'Can you make a lot of money doing accounts?'

'Why, no, not me. I don't earn anything, and I have to keep myself. But the thing is that you look about you. *That's* the great thing. Then the time comes when you see your opening. And you go in, and you make your money, and then there you are! When you have once made your money, you have nothing to do but use it.'

This was very like his way of fighting that day in the garden; very like. His manner of dealing with his poverty, too, was exactly like his manner when dealing with that defeat. It was evident that he had nothing around him but the simplest things of life, for everything that I remarked on turned out to have been sent in on my account from the coffee-house or somewhere else.

That Saturday evening we went for a walk in the streets of London, and we went half-price to the theatre; and next day we went to church at Westminster Abbey, and in the afternoon we walked in the parks.

On Monday afternoon we went to Mr Pocket's house at Hammersmith, where I was introduced to Mr and Mrs Pocket in their garden. Mr Pocket then took me into the house and showed me my room. Next he knocked at the doors of two other similar rooms, and introduced me to the men who lived there, by name Bentley Drummle and Startop. Drummle, an old-looking, heavily built young man, was whistling. Startop, younger in years and appearance, was reading and holding his head, as if he thought himself in danger of it exploding with too much knowledge.

After two or three days, when I had established myself in my room and had gone to London several times and ordered all I wanted from the shops, Mr Pocket and I had a long talk together. He knew more of my intended career than I knew myself, for he referred to his having been told by Mr Jaggers that I was not designed for any profession, and that I should be well enough educated if I could meet the standards of the average well-off young man. I agreed, of course, not knowing any better.

He advised me to attend certain places in London in order to acquire the knowledge I needed, and he was to be director of all my studies. He placed himself on confidential terms with me in an admirable manner, and I may state at once that he was always so honourable in carrying out his agreement with me, that he made me honourable in carrying out mine with him. If he had shown lack of interest as a master, I have no doubt I should have done the same as a pupil.

When these points were settled and I had begun to work hard, it occurred to me that if I could keep my bedroom in Barnard's Inn, my life would be pleasant, while my manners would be none the worse for Herbert's society. Mr Pocket did not object to this arrangement, but insisted that before any step could possibly be taken in it, I must ask my guardian. When I expressed this wish to Mr Jaggers he agreed, and ordered Wemmick to pay me twenty pounds to buy the necessary furniture.

Chapter 15   Joe Comes to Barnard's Inn

One Monday morning I received a letter from Biddy in which she told me of Joe's intention to visit me at Barnard's Inn the next morning. I did not look forward with pleasure to this visit, and if I could have kept him away by paying money, I certainly would have done so. It was a relief, however, to know that he was coming to my rooms in London and not to Mr Pocket's house at Hammersmith. I had little objection to his being seen by Herbert or his father, both of whom I respected, but I had the sharpest sensitivity to his being seen by Drummle, whom I held in contempt. So through our lives our worst weaknesses and meannesses are committed for the sake of people we least respect.

I got up early in the morning and made the sitting room and breakfast table look wonderful. Soon I heard Joe on the stairs.

I knew it was Joe by his heavy-footed manner of coming upstairs – his best boots being always too big for him – and by the time it took him to read the names on the other floors as he came up. Finally he gave a faint single knock and came in.

'Joe, how are you, Joe?'

'Pip, how are you, Pip?'

'I am glad to see you, Joe. Give me your hat.'

But Joe, taking it up carefully with both hands, like a bird's nest with eggs in it, wouldn't hear of parting with that piece of property, and stood talking over it in a most uncomfortable way.

'How you have grown,' he said, 'and got fat and become a gentleman! To be sure you are an honour to your king and country.'

'And you, Joe, look wonderfully well.'

'Thank God,' said Joe. 'Your sister is no worse than she was. And Biddy is always well, and ready to help. And all your friends are no worse, except Wopsle, who has left the church and gone into the play-acting.'

Soon Herbert entered the room, and I presented Joe to him. Herbert held out his hand, but Joe backed away from it, and held on to his hat.

'Your servant, sir. I hope you two gentlemen are finding this spot healthy. According to London opinion the place may be a very good one, but I wouldn't keep a pig in it myself – not if I wished it to grow healthy and fat.'

On being invited to sit down to table, he looked all round the room for a suitable spot on which to put his hat, and finally stood it on an extreme corner of the shelf above the fireplace, from which it fell off at intervals.

'Do you take tea or coffee, Mr Gargery?' asked Herbert.

'Thank you, sir,' said Joe, stiff from head to foot. 'I'll take whichever suits you.'

'What do you say to coffee?'

'Thank you, sir,' returned Joe, evidently not liking the idea; 'since you are so kind as to make choice of coffee, I will not go against your opinions. But don't you ever find it a little heating?'

'Say tea, then,' said Herbert, pouring it out.

Here Joe's hat fell off the shelf and he jumped out of his chair and picked it up, returning it to the exact same spot.

As to his shirt collar, and his coat collar, they were mysteries to reflect upon. Why should a man wear such tight, uncomfortable collars before he could consider himself well dressed? Why should he suppose it necessary to suffer for his holiday clothes? Then he fell into fits of deep thought with his fork halfway between his plate and his mouth, had such extraordinary coughs, sat so far from table, and dropped so much more than he ate, that I was extremely glad when Herbert left us for the City.

I had neither the good sense nor the good feeling to know that this was all my fault, and that if I had been easier with Joe, Joe would have been easier with me. I felt impatient and out of temper with him.

'We two being now alone, sir–' began Joe.

'Joe,' I interrupted, 'how can you call me sir?'

Joe looked at me for a single moment as if about to criticise me.

'We two being now alone,' he repeated, 'I will mention the cause of my visit. One evening, Pumblechook came to me and told me that Miss Havisham wished to speak to me. So next day I went and saw her. She asked if I was in touch with you, and when I replied that I was, she asked me to tell you that Estella had come home and would be glad to see you. I have now done that, sir,' said Joe, rising from his chair, 'and, Pip, I wish you ever well and ever rising to a greater and greater height.'

'But you are not going now, Joe?'

'Yes, I am,' said Joe.

'But you are coming back to dinner, Joe?'

'No, I am not,' said Joe.

Our eyes met, and all the 'sir' melted out of that manly heart as he gave me his hand.

'Pip, dear old chap, I'm wrong in these clothes. I'm wrong out of the forge, the kitchen, or off the marshes. You won't find half so much fault in me if you think of me in my forge dress, with my hammer in my hand, or even my pipe. You won't find half so much fault in me if, supposing you should ever wish to see me, you come and put your head in at the forge window and see Joe the blacksmith, there, sticking to the old work. So God keep you, dear old Pip, God keep you!'

There was a simple self-respect in him. He touched me gently on the forehead and went out. As soon as I could recover myself sufficiently, I hurried out after him and looked for him in the neighbouring streets; but he was gone.

Chapter 16   Estella Has No Heart

I took the afternoon coach to the town and arrived there late in the evening. I put up for the night at the local inn, and got up early the next morning to go to Miss Havisham's. It was too early yet to pay my visit, so I walked aimlessly into the country thinking about my benefactor and painting brilliant pictures of her plans for me. She had adopted Estella, she had as good as adopted me, and it could not fail to be her intention to bring us together. She intended me to restore the old house, admit the sunshine into the dark rooms, set the clocks going and the cold fireplaces burning – in short, do all the manly acts of a prince in a romantic story, and marry the princess.

I carefully timed my walk so as to arrive at the house at my old time. When I rang the bell, the gate was opened by the last man I should have expected to see there.

'Orlick!'

'Ah, young master, there are more changes than yours. But come in, come in. I'm not allowed to hold the gate open.'

I entered and he locked the gate and took the key out.

'How did you come here?'

'I came here,' he replied, 'on my legs.'

'Are you here for good?'

'I'm not here for harm, young master, I suppose.'

I was not so sure of that. I turned down the long passage and found Sarah Pocket, who led me to Miss Havisham's room.

'Come in Pip,' said Miss Havisham.

She was in her chair near the old table, in the old dress, with her two hands crossed on her stick. Sitting near her was a well-dressed lady whom I had never seen.

'Come in, Pip,' repeated Miss Havisham. 'How do you do, Pip? So you kiss my hand as if I were a queen, eh? Well?'

'I heard, Miss Havisham,' said I, 'that you were so kind as to wish me to come and see you, and I came directly.'

The lady whom I had never seen before lifted up her eyes and looked proudly at me, and then I saw that the eyes were Estella's eyes. But she was so much changed, so much more beautiful, so much more womanly, and had advanced so wonderfully that I seemed not to have improved at all. Before her I felt like the rough and common boy again.

She gave me her hand. I managed to say something about the pleasure I felt in seeing her again, and about my having looked forward to it for a long, long time.

'Do you find her much changed, Pip?' asked Miss Havisham with her hungry look, and striking her stick upon a chair that stood between them, as a sign to me to sit down there.

'When I came in, Miss Havisham, I thought there was nothing of Estella in the face or figure; but now it all settles down so strangely into the old–'

'What? You are not going to say into the old Estella?' Miss Havisham interrupted. 'She was proud and insulting, and you wanted to go away from her. Don't you remember?'

I said confusedly that that was long ago, and that I knew no better then, and other such things. Estella smiled with perfect calmness, and said she had no doubt of my having been quite right and of her having been very unpleasant.

'Is he changed?' Miss Havisham asked her.

'Very much,' said Estella, looking at me.

'Less rough and common?' said Miss Havisham, playing with Estella's hair.

Estella laughed and looked at me. She treated me as a boy still, but she lured me on.

It was settled that I should stay there all the rest of the day, and return to the hotel at night, and to London the next day. When we had talked for a while, Miss Havisham sent us out to walk in the overgrown garden. As we drew near to the place of my fight with the pale young gentleman, she stopped and said:

'I must have been a strange little creature to hide and see that fight that day; but I did, and I enjoyed it very much.'

I told her then that he and I were now great friends.

'Are you? I think I remember that you read with his father?'

'Yes,' I said, rather shyly, for it seemed to make me look boyish.

The grass was too long for walking in easily, and after we had gone round the garden two or three times, we came out again into the brewery yard. I reminded her where she had come out of the house and given me my meat and drink, and she said:

'I don't remember.'

'Not remember that you made me cry?' said I.

'No,' said she, and shook her head and looked around her. I believe that her not remembering and not caring in the least made me cry again, in my heart – and that is the sharpest crying of all.

'You must know,' said Estella, 'that I have no heart, no sympathy, no feeling.'

I told her I doubted that, and said there could be no such beauty without a heart.

'I am serious,' said Estella; 'if we are to be thrown much together, you had better believe it at once. Let us make one more round of the garden, and then go in. Come! You shall not cry for my cruelty today; you shall attend on me, and let me lean on your shoulder.'

She held her beautiful dress in one hand, and with the other lightly touched my shoulder as we walked. We walked round the garden two or three times more, and it all seemed in flower to me.

At last we went back into the house, and there I heard that my guardian had come down to see Miss Havisham on business, and would come back to dinner. Miss Havisham was in her chair and waiting for me. Then, Estella having gone to prepare herself for dinner, and we two being left alone, she turned to me and said in a whisper:

'Is she beautiful, graceful, well grown? Do you admire her?'

'Everybody must who sees her, Miss Havisham.'

She put her arm round my neck, and drew my head close down to hers as she sat in the chair.

'Love her, love her, love her!' she said to me. 'How does she treat you?'

Before I could answer (if I could have answered so difficult a question at all), she repeated, 'Love her, love her, love her! If she favours you, love her. If she wounds you, love her. If she tears your heart to pieces, love her, love her, love her! Hear me, Pip! I adopted her to be loved. I brought her up and educated her to be loved. Love her! I'll tell you what real love is. It is blind faithfulness, complete acceptance, trust and belief in spite of yourself and of the whole world, giving up your whole heart and soul to your love – as I did.'

On the last words she gave a wild cry, and rose up in her chair, and struck at the air as if she wanted to strike herself against the wall and fall dead.

In a surprisingly short space of time she was herself again, and soon Mr Jaggers entered the room. After a few words with Miss Havisham he took me away to have lunch with Estella and Miss Sarah Pocket. Miss Havisham remained sitting in her chair, for she never ate or drank in company. We ate very well, and after dinner a bottle of choice fine old wine was placed before my guardian, and the two ladies left us.

I have never seen anything to equal Mr Jaggers's reserve under that roof. He kept even his looks to himself and hardly directed his eyes to Estella's face once during dinner. When he and I were left alone, he made me feel very uncomfortable, and whenever he saw me going to ask him anything, he looked at me with his glass in his hand and rolling his wine about in his mouth, as if requesting me to take notice that it was of no use, for he couldn't answer.

Afterwards we went up to Miss Havisham's room and we played at cards. In the interval Miss Havisham had put some of the most beautiful jewels from her dressing table into Estella's hair, and round her neck and arms; and I saw even my guardian cast glances at her when her loveliness was before him.

We played until nine o'clock, and then it was arranged that when Estella came to London I should be warned of her coming and should meet her at the coach. I said goodnight to her, and returned to the inn.

Far into the night, Miss Havisham's words, 'Love her, love her, love her!' sounded in my ears. I changed them and repeated them in my own way hundreds of times, 'I love her, I love her, I love her!' Then a burst of thanks came upon me that she should be the one for me, once the blacksmith's boy. Then I wondered when she would begin to be interested in me. When should I wake the heart within her, that was sleeping now?

I thought those were high and great emotions. But I never thought there was anything low and small in my keeping away from Joe, because I knew she would hold him in contempt. Only the day before, Joe had brought the tears into my eyes; they had soon dried – God forgive me! – soon dried.

Chapter 17   I Open My Heart to Herbert

The next morning I told my guardian, who was staying at the inn with me, that I did not think Orlick the right sort of man to employ at Miss Havisham's. I told him what I knew of him. 'Very good, Pip,' he said, 'I'll go round soon, and pay him off.'

On my return to Barnard's Inn, I found Herbert eating a meal of cold meat and delighted to welcome me back. Having sent the servant boy to the coffee-house for food for me, I felt that I must tell my secret that very evening to my friend.

'My dear Herbert,' I began, 'I have something very particular to tell you.'

'My dear Handel,' he returned (he liked to call me Handel), 'I shall honour and respect your confidence.'

'It concerns myself, Herbert,' said I, 'and one other person.'

Herbert crossed his feet, looked at the fire with his head on one side, and having looked at it for some time, looked at me because I didn't go on.

'Herbert,' said I, laying my hand upon his knee, 'I love Estella with all my heart.'

Herbert replied in an easy, matter-of-fact way, 'Exactly. Well?'

'Well, Herbert. Is that all you say? Well?'

'What next, I mean?' said Herbert. 'Of course I know that.'

'How do you know it?' said I.

'How do I know it, Handel? Why, from you.'

'I never told you.'

'Told me! You have never told me when you have got your hair cut, but I have had senses to notice it. You have always loved her, ever since I have known you. You brought your love for her and your suitcase here, together. Told me! Why, you have always told me all day long. When you told me your own story, you told me plainly that you began loving her the first time you saw her, when you were very young indeed.'

'Very well then,' said I. 'I have never left off loving her. And she has come back, a most beautiful creature. And I saw her yesterday. And if I loved her before, I now love her with all my heart and soul.'

'Lucky for you then, Handel,' said Herbert, 'that you are picked out for her. Have you any idea yet of Estella's views on the matter?'

I shook my head sadly. 'Oh! she is thousands of miles away from me,' said I.

'Patience, my dear Handel: time enough, time enough. But you have something more to say?'

'I am ashamed to say it,' I returned, 'and yet it's no worse to say it than to think it. You call me a lucky fellow. Of course, I am. I was a blacksmith's boy only yesterday. I have done nothing to raise myself in life. Fortune alone has raised me. And yet, when I think of Estella, I cannot tell you how dependent and uncertain I feel, and how exposed to hundreds of chances. All my expectations depend on one person. And how indefinite and uncertain they are!'

'Didn't you tell me,' replied Herbert, 'that your guardian, Mr Jaggers, had told you in the beginning that you were not given expectations only? And even if he had not told you so, could you believe that of all men in London, Mr Jaggers is the man to maintain his present relationship with you, unless he were sure of his ground?'

I said I could not deny that this was a strong point.

'I should think it was a strong point,' said Herbert; 'as to the rest, you must give your guardian time, and he must give his client time. You'll be one-and-twenty before you know where you are, and then perhaps you'll get some further information. And now I want to make myself seriously unpleasant to you for a moment. I have been thinking that Estella cannot be a condition of your good fortune, if she was never mentioned by your protector. Has he never suggested, for instance, that your benefactor might have views regarding your marriage?'

'Never.'

'Now, Handel. Not being engaged to her, can you not take yourself from her?'

'I can't help it, Herbert.'

'You can't stop wanting her?'

'No. Impossible!'

'Well,' said Herbert, 'now I'll try to make myself pleasant again.' Then he told me about his family, and especially about himself. He was engaged to a young lady, called Clara, who lived in London, and whose father was very old, always keeping to his room, and making a tremendous row in it.

Herbert told me that the moment he began to make money it was his intention to marry this young lady. 'But you can't marry, you know,' he added, 'while you're looking around you.'

Chapter 18   I Take Estella to Richmond

One day I received a note by post, the mere outside of which caused me great pleasure for, though I had never seen the handwriting in which it was addressed, I guessed whose hand it was. It ran thus:

I am to come to London the day after tomorrow by the midday coach. I believe it was settled you should meet me. At all events Miss Havisham has that impression, and I write in obedience to it. She sends you her regards.

Yours,

ESTELLA.

If there had been time, I should probably have ordered several suits of clothes for this occasion, but as there was not, I had to be content with those I had. Suddenly I could eat nothing, and I had no peace until the day arrived; nor had I any peace then, for I began waiting at the coach office before the coach had left its point of departure. It arrived at last, and I saw Estella's face at the coach window and her hand waving to me.

In her travelling dress, Estella seemed more delicately beautiful than she had ever seemed yet, even in my eyes. Her manner was more winning than she had cared to let it be to me before, and I thought I saw Miss Havisham's influence in the change.

We stood in the coach-office yard while she pointed out her luggage to me, and when it was all collected I remembered – having forgotten everything but herself in the meanwhile – that I knew nothing of where she was going.

'I am going to Richmond,' she told me. 'The distance is ten miles. I am to have a carriage, and you are to take me. This is my purse, and you are to pay my charges out of it. Oh, you must take the purse. We have no choice, you and I, but to obey our instructions.'

'A carriage will have to be sent for, Estella. Will you rest here a little?'

'Yes, I am to rest here a little, and I am to drink some tea, and you are to take care of me.'

She drew her arm through mine, as if it must be done, and I requested a waiter who had been staring at the coach like a man who had never seen such a thing in his life, to show us a private sitting room. He led us to a room upstairs, and I ordered tea for Estella.

'Where are you going to at Richmond?' I asked her.

'I am going to live,' she said, 'at a great expense, with a lady there, called Mrs Brandley, who has the power of taking me about, and introducing me, and showing people to me and showing me to people.'

'I suppose you will be glad of variety and admiration?'

'Yes, I suppose so. Are you happy with Mr Herbert Pocket?'

'I live quite pleasantly there; at least as pleasantly as I could anywhere, away from you.'

'You silly boy,' said Estella, quite calmly. 'How can you talk such nonsense? Your friend Mr Matthew Pocket, I believe, is in a higher position than the rest of his family?'

'Oh yes.'

'He really is kind and above small jealousy and hatred, I have heard?'

'I am sure I have every reason to say so.'

'You have not every reason to say so of the rest of his people,' said Estella, 'for they keep sending to Miss Havisham reports to your disadvantage. You can hardly realize the hatred those people feel for you.'

'They do me no harm, I hope?'

Instead of answering, Estella burst out laughing.

'I hope,' I said, 'you would not be amused if they did me any harm?'

'No, no, you may be sure of that,' said Estella. 'You may be certain that I laugh because they fail. Oh, those people with Miss Havisham, and the hardships they put up with from her!' She laughed again and her laughter seemed too much for the occasion, and I thought there must really be something more here than I knew.

'You may set your mind at rest,' added Estella, 'that these people never will – never would in a hundred years – weaken your position with Miss Havisham. And besides, I am in debt to you as the cause of their being so busy and so mean with no hope of success, and there is my hand on it.'

As she gave it me playfully, I held it and put it to my lips.

'You ridiculous boy,' said Estella. 'Will you never take warning? Or do you kiss my hand in the same spirit in which I once let you kiss my cheek?'

'What spirit was that?' said I.

'I must think a moment. A spirit of contempt for those who seek Miss Havisham's favour.'

'If I say yes, may I kiss the cheek again?'

'You should have asked before you touched the hand. But, yes, if you like.'

I leaned down, and her calm face was stone. 'Now,' said Estella, moving away as soon as I touched her cheek, 'you are to take care that I have some tea, and you are to take me to Richmond.'

I rang for the tea. This having been brought and drunk, and the bill paid, we got into our coach and drove away. When we passed through Hammersmith, I showed her where Mr Matthew Pocket lived, and said it was no great way from Richmond, and that I hoped I should see her sometimes.

'Oh, yes, you are to see me; you are to come when you think proper; you are to be mentioned to the family; indeed you are already mentioned.'

We came to Richmond all too soon, and the house where we stopped was old and respectable. At the door there appeared, when I had rung the bell, two servants who came to receive Estella. She gave me her hand and a smile, and said good night and disappeared within. And still I stood looking at the house, thinking how happy I should be if I lived there with her, and knowing that I never was happy with her, but always sad.

Chapter 19   We Fall into Debt

As I had grown used to my expectations I had begun to notice their effect upon myself and those around me. I lived in a state of continual anxiety regarding my behaviour to Joe. And I was not by any means comfortable about my behaviour to Biddy. When I woke up in the night I used to think, with a tiredness of my spirits, that I should have been happier and better if I had never seen Miss Havisham's face, and had grown up content to be Joe's partner in the honest old forge.

The influence of my new position was not of benefit to Herbert. My expensive lifestyle led him into expenses that he could not afford, spoilt the simplicity of his life, and upset his peace with worries.

I began to get into debt, and Herbert soon followed.

I would willingly have taken Herbert's expenses on myself; but Herbert was proud, and I could make no such suggestion to him. So, he got into difficulties in every way, and continued to look around him.

Every morning he went into the City;* and I often paid him a visit in his office, but I do not remember that I ever saw him do anything but look around him.

Sometimes I would say to him, 'My dear Herbert, we are getting on badly.'

'My dear Handel,' Herbert would say to me, 'if you will believe me, those very words were on my lips.'

'Then, Herbert,' I would say, 'let us look into our affairs.'

We always took great satisfaction in making an appointment for this purpose. We ordered something special for dinner, with an expensive bottle of wine, in order that our minds might be strengthened for the occasion. Dinner over, we produced pens

*the City: an area of central London which is Britian's financial centre

and paper. I would then take a sheet of paper and write across the top of it, in a neat handwriting, 'A List of Pip's Debts'. Herbert would also take a sheet of paper and write across it, 'A List of Herbert's Debts'. Each of us would then refer to a confused pile of papers at his side, which had been thrown into drawers, worn into holes in pockets, half-burnt in lighting candles, stuck for weeks into the mirror, and otherwise damaged. The sound of our pens going made us feel good, so much so that I sometimes found it difficult to distinguish between writing our lists and actually paying the money.

When we had written a little while, I would ask Herbert how he got on. 'They are increasing, Handel,' he would say; 'on my life, they are increasing.'

'Be firm, Herbert,' I would reply. 'Look the thing in the face. Look into your affairs.'

My determined manner would have its effect, and Herbert would fall to work again. After a time he would give up once more, making the excuse that some of the bills were missing.

'Then Herbert, estimate; estimate it in round numbers and put it down.'

'What a clever fellow you are!' my friend would reply, with admiration. 'Really your business powers are amazing.'

I thought so too. I considered myself on these occasions a first-rate man of business, firm, clear, cool-headed.

One of my business habits was what I called Leaving a Margin. For example: supposing Herbert's debts to be one hundred and sixty-four pounds, I would say, 'Leave a margin, and put them down at two hundred.' Or supposing my own to be four times as much, I would leave a margin, and put them down at seven hundred. I had the highest opinion of the wisdom of this margin, but I have to say that it was an expensive device. For we always ran into new debts immediately, to the full extent of the margin, and sometimes got pretty far on into another margin.

But there was a calm, a rest, resulting from these examinations of our affairs, that gave me, for the time, an admirable opinion of myself. I had fallen into this calm state one evening, when a letter from Biddy arrived, informing me of the death of my sister, and requesting that I should attend the burial next Monday.

I could hardly have remembered my sister with much warmth. But I suppose there is a shock of sadness which may exist without much warmth. Under its influence, I was seized with a violent anger against the attacker from whom she had suffered so much, and I felt that had there been sufficient proof, I could have pursued Orlick, or anyone else, to the ends of the earth.

I wrote to Joe and, when the day arrived, I took the coach to my village and walked over to the forge.

The funeral over, Joe, Biddy and I had a cold dinner together. Joe was much pleased by my asking if I might sleep in my own little room. When the shadows of evening were closing in, I took an opportunity of getting into the garden with Biddy for a little walk.

'I suppose it will be difficult for you to remain here now, Biddy dear?' I said to her.

'Oh! I can't do so, Mr Pip,' said Biddy in a tone of sadness. 'I have been speaking to Mrs Hubble, and I am going to her tomorrow. I hope we shall be able to take some care of Mr Gargery together, until he settles down.'

'How are you going to live, Biddy? If you want any mo–'

'How am I going to live? I'll tell you, Mr Pip. I am going to try to get the place of teacher in the new school nearly finished here. I learnt a good deal from you, Mr Pip; and have had time since then to improve.'

'I think you would always improve, Biddy, under any circumstances.' Then she told me the details of my sister's death. She had been in one of her bad states for four days when she came out of it in the evening, and said quite plainly, 'Joe.' Joe was called from the forge and she made signs that she wanted him to sit down close to her, and she laid her head down on his shoulder, quite content and satisfied. After a while she said 'Joe' again and 'Pardon', and once 'Pip'. And she never lifted her head up again, and an hour later she was gone.

'Nothing was ever discovered, Biddy?'

'Nothing.'

'Do you know what has happened to Orlick?'

'I should think, from the colour of his clothes, that he is working in the quarries.'

Then she told me that he was still trying to make love to her, which made me very angry.

Early in the morning, I was to go. Early in the morning, I was out and looking in, unseen, at one of the windows of the forge. There I stood, for minutes, looking at Joe already at work with a look of health and strength upon his face.

'Goodbye, dear Joe! No, don't wipe it off – for God's sake, give me your blackened hand! – I shall be here again and often.'

'Never too soon, sir,' said Joe, 'and never too often, Pip.'

Chapter 20   I Come of Age

Herbert and I went from bad to worse, in the way of increasing our debts, looking into our affairs, leaving margins and the like; and time went on and I came of age. On the day before my twenty-first birthday, I received an official note from Wemmick, informing me that Mr Jaggers would be glad if I would call on him at five in the afternoon of the next day.

When I arrived at the outer office, Wemmick offered me his congratulations, and motioned me into my guardian's room.

Mr Jaggers shook hands with me, calling me Mr Pip, this time, and congratulated me. Then he asked me how much I was spending, but I was unable to answer that question.

I asked him if my benefactor was to be made known to me that day. He answered that he was not. Then he said that he knew I was in debt, and gave me a bank note for five hundred pounds. He added that I was to receive such a sum of money annually, and I was to live at this rate until my benefactor appeared. I was beginning to express my thanks to my benefactor for the great generosity with which I was treated, when Mr Jaggers stopped me. 'I am not paid, Pip,' said he, coolly, 'to carry your words to anyone.' I made repeated efforts to find out when the name of my secret benefactor was to be revealed, and whether he (or she) was coming to London, but they all failed. All I could get Mr Jaggers to say was this: 'When that person reveals himself to you, my part in the business will cease.' From this I concluded that Miss Havisham, for some reason or other, had not told him about her wishes regarding Estella and me; that he was angry about this and felt a jealousy about it; or that he really did object to the scheme, and would have nothing to do with it.

I left him and went into Wemmick's office. The five hundred pounds in my pocket gave me an idea, and I wanted to ask Wemmick's advice.

I told him that I wanted to help a friend who was trying to get on in commercial life but had no money. Mr Wemmick's opinion was that such a thing would be a foolish thing to do, and that it would be as good as throwing one's money into the Thames.

But Wemmick at home was a kinder man than Wemmick in the office, and so I called on him several times at his home, and finally we found a young merchant, Clarriker by name, who wanted intelligent help and money, and in due time would want a partner. Between him and me a secret agreement, of which Herbert was the subject, was signed, and I paid him half of my five hundred pounds, and promised to make different other payments at certain dates out of my income.

The whole business was so cleverly managed that Herbert had not the least idea of my hand being in it. I never shall forget the smiling face with which he came home one afternoon and told me, as a mighty piece of news, of his having come across a young merchant who had shown an extraordinary liking for him, and of his belief that the opening had come at last. Day by day his hopes grew stronger and his face brighter, until at last the thing was done and he entered the business. I cried for joy when I went to bed, to think that my expectations had done some good to somebody.

Chapter 21   Estella and Miss Havisham Opposed

If that respectable old house at Richmond should ever have a ghost after I am dead, it will surely be me. Oh the many, many nights and days my restless spirit walked around that house when Estella lived there!

In and out of that house I suffered every kind of pain that Estella could cause me. The nature of my relations with her, which placed me on terms of familiarity without placing me on terms of favour, nearly drove me mad. She used me to play games with other admirers, and she had admirers without end. I saw her often at Richmond, I heard of her often in town, and I used often to take her and the Brandleys, with whom she was staying, to plays, concerts, parties and all sorts of pleasures, through which I pursued her – but all these occasions brought me sadness. I never had one hour's happiness in her society, and yet my mind all round the four-and-twenty hours kept thinking of the happiness of having her with me until death.

One evening she told me that Miss Havisham wished to have

her for a day at Satis House, and that I was to take her there and bring her back if I would. I willingly agreed, and we went down on the next day but one, and found Miss Havisham in the room where I had first seen her.

She was even more fond of Estella than she had been when I last saw them together. She was overcome by her beauty, amazed by her words and movements, and looked at her as if she were hungrily eating the beautiful creature she had brought up.

From Estella she looked at me, with a searching glance. 'How does she treat you, Pip, how does she treat you?' she asked me again, eagerly, even in Estella's hearing. But when we sat by her fire at night, she was most strange; for then, keeping Estella's hand drawn through her arm and held in her hand, she made her mention the names and conditions of the men whom she had attracted; and as Miss Havisham fixed her attention upon this list, she sat with her other hand on her stick, and stared at me like a ghost.

I saw in this that Estella was set to work to take Miss Havisham's revenge on men, and that she was not to be given to me until the revenge was complete. I saw in this the reason for my being put off so long, and the reason for Mr Jaggers's refusal to admit any knowledge of her being reserved for me.

It happened on the occasion of this visit that some sharp words were said between Estella and Miss Havisham. It was the first time I had ever seen them opposed.

We were seated by the fire, and Miss Havisham still had Estella's arm drawn through her own, when Estella gradually began to pull herself away.

'What!' said Miss Havisham, flashing her eyes at her. 'Are you tired of me?'

'Only a little tired of myself,' replied Estella, freeing her arm, and moving to the chimney piece, where she stood looking down at the fire.

'Speak the truth, you ungrateful person!' cried Miss Havisham, angrily striking her stick on the floor. 'You are tired of me.'

Estella looked at her with perfect calmness, and again looked down at the fire.

'You stone!' exclaimed Miss Havisham. 'You cold, cold heart!'

'What!' said Estella. 'Do you blame me for being cold? You?'

'Are you not?' was the fierce reply.

'You should know,' said Estella. 'I am what you have made me. Take all the praise, take all the blame; take all the success, take all the failure; in short, take me.'

'Oh, look at her, look at her!' cried Miss Havisham, bitterly. 'Look at her, so hard and thankless, in the home where she was brought up! Where I took her into my heart when it was first bleeding, and where I have spent years of loving care on her!'

'What would you have?' said Estella. 'You have been very good to me, and I owe everything to you. What would you have?'

'Love,' replied the other.

'You have it.'

'I have not,' said Miss Havisham.

'Mother by adoption, I have said that I owe everything to you. All I possess is freely yours. All that you have given me is at your command to have again. Beyond that, I have nothing. And if you ask me to give you what you never gave me, that is impossible.'

'Did I never give her love!' cried Miss Havisham, turning wildly to me. 'Did I never give her a burning love, while she speaks thus to me! Let her call me mad, let her call me mad!'

'Why should I call you mad,' returned Estella, 'I, of all people? Does anyone live who knows what purposes you have, half as well as I do? Does anyone live who knows what a steady memory you have, half as well as I do? I who have sat in this same room learning your lessons and looking up into your face, when your face was strange and frightened me!'

'Soon forgotten!' cried Miss Havisham. 'Times soon forgotten!'

'No, not forgotten,' replied Estella. 'Not forgotten, but held close in my memory. When have you found me false to your teaching? When have you found me giving admission here,' she touched her breast with her hand, 'to anything that you did not like? Be just to me.'

'So proud, so proud!' whispered Miss Havisham.

'Who taught me to be proud?' returned Estella. 'Who praised me when I learnt my lesson?'

'So hard, so hard!' cried Miss Havisham.

'Who taught me to be hard?' returned Estella. 'Who praised me when I learnt my lesson?'

'But to be proud and hard to me!' Miss Havisham cried, as she stretched out her arms. 'Estella, Estella, to be proud and hard to me!'

Estella looked at her with calm wonder; then she looked at the fire again. I took advantage of the moment to leave the room, and walked in the starlight for an hour or more in the ruined garden. When I at last took courage to return to the room, I found Estella sitting at Miss Havisham's knee. Afterwards Estella and I played at cards, once again, and so the evening wore away, and I went to bed.

Before we left next day, there was no return to the quarrel between Miss Havisham and Estella, nor was it returned to on any similar occasion.

◆

It is impossible to turn this page of my life without putting Bentley Drummle's name upon it; or I would very gladly.

On a certain occasion when Herbert and I, together with some friends, were gathered in our club, I thought I saw Bentley look at me and laugh in an ugly way. Soon he called on the company to drink to the health of Estella.

'Estella who?' said I.

'Never you mind,' replied Drummle.

'Estella of where?' said I.

'Of Richmond, gentlemen,' said Drummle, 'and a beauty without equal.'

'I know that lady,' said Herbert, across the table.

'*Do* you?' said Drummle.

'And so do I,' I added with a red face.

'*Do you?*' said Drummle. 'Oh, Lord!'

This filled me with anger; I called him a rude fellow for daring to talk of a lady of whom he knew nothing, and I expressed my readiness to fight with him. But the company decided that if Mr Drummle would bring a certificate from the lady to the effect that he knew her, I must express my apologies, as a gentleman, for having lost my temper. Next day Drummle appeared with a little note, in Estella's handwriting, saying that she had had the honour of dancing with him several times. This left me no course but to apologize.

I cannot express what pain it gave me to think that Estella should show any favour to such a terrible fellow. So I took the first opportunity of meeting her at a ball at Richmond to speak to her about this matter. Drummle was there.

'Estella,' said I, 'do look at that fellow in the corner, who is looking at us.'

'Why should I look at him?' returned Estella. 'What is there in him that I need look at?'

'Indeed, that is the very question I want to ask you,' said I. 'For he has been hanging around you all night.'

'All sorts of insects,' replied Estella, with a glance towards him, 'are drawn to a lighted candle. Can the candle help it?'

'No, but Estella, it makes me sad that you should encourage a man so badly regarded as Drummle. I have seen you give him looks and smiles this very night, such as you never give to me.'

'Do you want me, then,' said Estella, 'to deceive and trap you?'

'Do you deceive and trap him, Estella?'

'Yes, and many others − all of them but you. Here is Mrs Brandley. I'll say no more.'

Chapter 22   My Strange Visitor

I was twenty-three years of age. Herbert and I had left Barnard's Inn more than a year before, and now lived in the Temple.* Our chambers were in Garden Court, down by the river. Business had taken Herbert on a journey to Marseilles, and I was alone. I missed the cheerful face and company of my friend, and sat reading until eleven o'clock. As I shut the book, I heard a footstep on the stair. I took up my reading lamp and went out to the top of the stairs.

'There is someone down there, is there not?' I called out, looking down.

'Yes,' said a voice from the darkness beneath.

'Which floor do you want?'

'The top − Mr Pip.'

'That is my name.'

The man came up. By the shaded light of my reading lamp I saw a face that was strange to me, looking up with an air of being touched and pleased by the sight of me.

Moving the lamp as the man moved, I made out that he was dressed like a man who had been travelling by sea. He had long, iron-grey hair, and his age was about sixty. He was a strong man,

*the Temple: an area of central London in which a number of buildings belong to lawyer's societies.

browned and hardened by the weather. As he came up the last stair or two, I saw that he was holding out both his hands to me.

'What is your business?' I asked him.

'My business?' he repeated, pausing. 'Ah! Yes. I will explain my business, with your permission.'

'Do you wish to come in?'

'Yes,' he replied, 'I wish to come in, master.'

I took him into the room I had just left, and asked him to explain himself.

He looked about him with wondering pleasure, as if he had some part in the things he admired, and he pulled off a rough outer coat and his hat, and once more held out both his hands to me.

'What do you want?' said I, half suspecting him to be mad.

He sat down on a chair that stood before the fire, and covered his forehead with his large brown hands.

'There is no one near,' said he, looking over his shoulder, 'is there?'

'Why do you, a stranger coming into my rooms at this time of the night, ask that question?' said I.

'You're a brave young man,' he returned, shaking his head at me affectionately; 'I'm glad you've grown up a brave young man! But don't catch hold of me. You'd be sorry afterwards to have done it.'

I gave up the intention he had detected, for I knew him! I knew my convict from the marshes! No need to take a file from his pocket and show it to me. No need to take the cloth from his neck and twist it round his head. I had recognized him even before he gave me those aids.

He came back to where I stood, and again held out both his hands. Not knowing what to do, I slowly gave him my hands. He took them firmly, raised them to his lips, kissed them, and still held them.

'You acted nobly, my boy,' said he. 'Noble Pip! And I have never forgotten it.'

He was going to put his arms around me, but I pushed him away.

'Keep off!' said I. 'If you are grateful to me for what I did when I was a little child, I hope you have shown your thanks by mending your way of life. You are wet, and you look tired. Will you drink something before you go?'

He said that he would. I made him some hot whisky-and-water, and as I gave it to him, I saw with surprise that his eyes were full of tears. I was softened by this, and, hurriedly pouring myself a drink, said to him: 'I am sorry I spoke in this way to you just now. I wish you well and happy. How are you living?'

'I've been a sheep farmer, cattle man, other trades besides, away in the New World,' said he.

'I hope you have done well?'

'I've done wonderfully well.'

'I am glad to hear it.'

'May I ask,' he said, 'how you have done, since we met on the marshes?'

I began to tremble. I forced myself to tell him that I had been chosen to succeed to some property.

'Might I ask whose property?'

I stopped, 'I don't know.'

'Could I make a guess, I wonder,' said the man, 'at your income since you came of age? As to the first figure, now. Five? Concerning a guardian. Some lawyer maybe. As to the first letter of that lawyer's name, now. Would it be J? It might be Jaggers.'

Then he told me, to my complete amazement, that he was my benefactor, that he had come over the sea to Portsmouth, and obtained my address from Wemmick. He had made a gentleman of me! He had lived rough so I might live smooth. He had worked hard so that I might be above work.

He knelt before me and called me his son. He had worked on

a farm looking after the sheep and had sworn that every pound he got would be mine. His master had died and left him money; and then he worked on his own and became rich, and made a gentleman of me.

He laid his hand on my shoulder. The thought that for all I knew, his hands might have blood on them, filled me with horror.

'Where will you put me?' he asked, after a while.

'To sleep?' said I.

'Yes. And to sleep long and sound,' he answered; 'for I've been at sea for many months.'

'My friend,' said I, 'is absent; you must have his room.'

'He won't come back tomorrow, will he?'

'No,' said I, 'not tomorrow.'

'Because, look here, dear boy, we must be careful.'

'How do you mean? Careful?'

'It's death: I was sent for life. It's death to come back.'

My first care was to close the curtains, so that no light might be seen from outside, and then to close and lock the doors. Then I lent him some of my bedclothes and he went to bed.

I sat down by the fire, afraid to go to bed myself. For an hour or more, I remained too surprised to think; and it was not until I began to think that I began fully to know how wrecked I was, and how the ship in which I had sailed had gone to pieces.

Miss Havisham's intentions towards me, all a mere dream; Estella not designed for me; I only suffered in Satis House as a sting for the greedy relations. Those were the first pains I had. But, sharpest and deepest pain of all – it was for this man, guilty of I knew not what crimes, and likely to be hanged, that I had deserted Joe and Biddy.

This is the end of the second stage of Pip's expectations.

Chapter 23   Provis and Compeyson

I had a restless night, sleeping in front of the fire. I woke up at six, and then fell into a deep sleep, from which the daylight suddenly woke me. I washed and dressed, and sat by the fire waiting for – Him – to come to breakfast.

Soon his door opened and he came out. I could not bring myself to bear the sight of him, and I thought he had a worse look by daylight.

He told me that he had taken the name of Provis on board the ship, but his real name was Abel Magwitch.

After breakfast – and he ate hungrily – he began to smoke his pipe, and then took out of his pocket a great thick pocketbook, bursting with papers, and threw it on the table.

'There is something worth spending in that book, dear boy. It's yours. All I've got is yours.'

'I want to speak to you,' said I. 'I want to know what is to be done. I want to know how you are to be kept out of danger.'

'Well, dear boy,' he said, 'the danger is not so great, unless someone informs the police.'

'And how long do you remain?'

'How long?' said he. 'I'm not going back.'

'Where are you to live?' said I. 'What is to be done with you? Where will you be safe?'

'Dear boy,' he returned, 'there are hair pieces, and hair powder, and glasses, and black clothes and all kinds of things. I can make myself look different. As to where and how I am to live, give me your opinions of it.'

It appeared to me that I could do no better than find some quiet room nearby for him, of which he might take possession when Herbert returned. That the secret must be told to Herbert was plain to me.

I persuaded Provis to dress in the clothes of a well-off farmer;

and we arranged that he should cut his hair short, and put a little powder on it. He was to keep himself out of my servants' view until his change of dress was made.

I was fortunate to secure for him the second floor of a respectable boarding-house nearby. I went from shop to shop, buying the necessary clothes, and next day he put them on. Whatever he put on suited him less than what he had worn before. To my thinking there was something in him that made it hopeless to attempt to make him look different. He dragged one of his legs as if there were still a weight of iron on it. Besides, his previous lonely life gave him a wild air that no dress could hide. In all his ways of sitting and standing, and eating and drinking, there was Convict, plain as plain could be.

All the time I was expecting Herbert, and I dared not go out except when I took Provis to get some air after dark. Finally, one evening, I heard Herbert's welcome footstep on the stair. He came bursting in, fresh from his journey to France.

'Handel, my dear fellow, how are you, and again how are you? I seem to have been gone a whole year! Why, so I must have been, for you have grown quite thin and pale! Handel, my – Hello! I beg your pardon.'

'Herbert, my dear friend,' said I, shutting the door, 'something very strange has happened. This is a visitor of mine.'

'It's all right, dear boy!' said Provis, coming forward with a dirty little black Bible he had taken out of his pocket. 'Take it in your right hand. Lord strike you dead on the spot if ever you give me away. Kiss it!'

'Do so, as he wishes it,' I said to Herbert. So Herbert, looking at me with a friendly anxiety and surprise, did as he was asked. Then we all sat down by the fire, and I told him the whole of the secret.

We sat up late. It was midnight before I took Provis round to his rooms, and saw him safely in. When the door closed upon him, I experienced the first moment of relief I had known since his arrival.

Back in my flat, I sat down with Herbert to consider the question, What was to be done?

'Herbert,' said I, 'something must be done. He wants to buy more things – horses and carriages and other expensive things. He must be stopped somehow.'

'You mean you can't accept?'

'How can I?' I interrupted, as Herbert paused. 'Think of him! Look at him! Think what a life he has led!'

We looked at each other.

'Yet I am afraid the awful truth is, Herbert, that he is attached to me, strongly attached to me. Was there ever such a problem! Then, think what I owe him already. And I am heavily in debt – very heavily for me, who have now no expectations – and I have been brought up to no trade or profession, and I am fit for nothing, except perhaps for being a soldier.'

'Soldiering won't do,' returned Herbert. 'You wouldn't be able to repay what you owe him. Besides, it's mad. You would be far better in Clarriker's house, small as it is. I am working up towards a partnership, you know.'

Poor fellow! He little suspected with whose money.

'But the first and the main thing to be done,' Herbert went on, 'is to get him out of England. You will have to go with him, and then he may be persuaded to go.'

The next morning he came to breakfast, and I asked him to tell us more about himself and about the other convict with whom he had struggled on the marshes.

After reminding Herbert that he had sworn to keep the secret, he consented. This is, in brief, what he told us:

'I've no more idea of where I was born than you have. I first became aware of myself, down in Essex, stealing vegetables for my living. Everyone who saw me, hungry and poor, drove me off or took me away. I was put in prison so often that I became hardened to it. I practically lived in prison. Begging, stealing, working sometimes when I could, doing a bit of most things that don't pay and lead to trouble, I got to be a man.

'Then at Epsom races, more than 20 years ago, I met a man whose head I'd crack open if I could find him now. His name was Compeyson; and that's the man, dear Pip, whom you saw me struggling with that time on the marshes. He pretended to be a gentleman, this Compeyson, and he'd been to a good school and had learning. He was a smooth talker, and good-looking too. He persuaded me to be a partner with him in his business of cheating, passing stolen bank notes, and suchlike. All sorts of traps as he could set with his head, and keep his own legs out of, and get the profits from and blame another man for, were Compeyson's business. He'd no more heart than an iron file, he was as cold as death, and he was as evil as the Devil.

'We soon got busy, and he got me into such traps as made me his slave. I was always in debt to him, always under his thumb, always working for him, always getting into danger. At last we were both tried on a charge of circulating stolen bank notes, and there were other charges too.

'The jury recommended a lighter sentence for Compeyson on account of good character and bad company, and because he gave up all the information he could against me. He was given seven years in prison, and I fourteen.

'We were in the same prison ship, but I couldn't get at him for long, though I tried. At last I came behind him and hit him on the cheek to turn him round and get a proper blow at him, when I was seen and seized. I managed to escape from the ship and hid among the graves near the shore, and there I first saw my boy!

'From you, my dear boy, I learnt that Compeyson was out on the marshes too. I believe he escaped in terror of me, not knowing that I had got on to land. I hunted him down. I hit him in his face. Caring nothing for myself, I decided to drag him back to the prison ship, as the worst thing I could do to him, when the soldiers came and seized us both. I was put in irons, brought to trial again, and sent away for life. I didn't stay away for life, dear boy and Pip's friend, as you now see me here.'

'Is he dead?' I asked after a silence.

'He hopes *I* am, if he's alive, you may be sure. I never heard any more of him.'

Herbert had been writing in the cover of a book. He softly pushed the book over to me, as Provis stood smoking with his eyes on the fire, and I read in it:

'Compeyson is the man who pretended to be Miss Havisham's lover.'

I shut the book and nodded slightly to Herbert, but we neither of us said anything, and both looked at Provis as he stood smoking by the fire.

Chapter 24   Miss Havisham's Revenge

I resolved to see Estella and Miss Havisham before I went abroad with Provis. So I went to Richmond the next day, but the servant told me that Estella had gone to Satis House.

I set off, early the next morning, for the town. When the coach drove up to the inn I saw Bentley Drummle come out. It was poisonous to me to see him in the town, for I knew very well why he had come there.

We both went into the coffee room, where he had just finished his breakfast, and where I had ordered mine. It was a most disagreeable meeting. He called the waiter and said to him:

'Is that horse of mine ready?'

'Brought round to the door, sir.'

'Look here. The lady won't ride today; the weather won't do.'

'Very good, sir.'

'And I will not be eating because I am going to eat at the lady's.'

'Very good, sir.'

Then Drummle glanced at me, with a smile of contempt on his face that cut me to the heart. It was a relief when he was gone.

I washed and dressed and went to Satis House. Miss Havisham was sitting near the fire, and Estella at her feet, sewing.

I told Miss Havisham that I had found out who my benefactor was, and she admitted having led me on when I fell into the mistake of thinking that it was she.

'Was that kind?' I said.

'Who am I,' cried Miss Havisham, striking her stick upon the floor and flashing suddenly into anger, 'who am I, for God's sake, that I should be kind?'

Then I turned to Estella.

'Estella,' said I, 'you know I love you. You know that I have loved you long and dearly.'

She raised her eyes to my face, on being thus addressed, and her fingers went on sewing, and she looked at me unmoved.

'I should have said this sooner, but for my long mistake in thinking that Miss Havisham meant us for one another. While I thought you could not help yourself, I prevented myself from saying it. But I must say it now.'

Still unmoved, and still sewing, Estella shook her head.

'I know,' said I, in answer to that action; 'I know. I have no hope that I shall ever call you mine, Estella. Still I love you. I have loved you ever since I first saw you in this house.'

Looking at me perfectly unmoved and with her fingers busy, she shook her head again. Then she said, very calmly: 'It seems that there are emotions which I am unable to understand. When you say you love me, I know what you mean, as a form of words, but nothing more. You address nothing in my breast, you touch nothing there. I don't care for what you say at all. I have tried to warn you of this; now, have I not ?'

I said sadly, 'Yes.'

'Yes. But you would not be warned, for you thought I did not mean it. Now, did you not think so?'

'I thought and hoped you could not mean it. You, so young, inexperienced, and beautiful. Estella! Surely it is not in Nature.'

'It is in my nature,' she returned; 'it is in the nature formed within me.'

Then I asked her whether it was true that she encouraged Bentley Drummle, that she rode out with him, and that he was to eat with her that same day.

She seemed a little surprised that I should know it, but replied, 'Quite true.'

'You cannot love him, Estella?'

'What have I told you? Do you still think, in spite of it, that I do not mean what I say?'

'You would never marry him, Estella?'

She looked towards Miss Havisham, and considered for a moment, with her work in her hands. Then she said, 'Why not tell you the truth? I am going to be married to him.'

I dropped my face into my hands, but was able to control myself better than I could have expected, considering what unhappiness it gave me to hear her say those words.

'Estella, dearest, dearest Estella, do not let Miss Havisham lead you into this fatal step. Put me aside for ever – you have done so, I well know – but give yourself to some worthier person than Drummle. Miss Havisham gives you to him as the greatest insult and injury that could be done to the many far better men who admire you, and to the few who truly love you.'

'I am going,' she said, in a gentler voice, 'to be married to him. The preparations for my marriage are being made, and I shall be married soon. Why do you bring in the name of my mother by adoption? It is my own act.'

'Your own act, Estella, to throw yourself away upon an animal? Such a mean, stupid animal?'

'Don't be afraid of my being a comfort to him,' said Estella; 'I shall not be that. Come! Here is my hand. Do we part on this, you silly boy – or man?'

'Oh Estella!' I answered, as my bitter tears fell fast on her hand. 'How can I think of you as Drummle's wife?'

'Nonsense,' she returned, 'nonsense. This will pass in no time.'

'Never, Estella!'

'You will get me out of your thoughts in a week.'

'Out of my thoughts! You are part of my existence, part of myself. Oh God keep you, God forgive you!'

All done, all gone! So much was done and gone, that when I went out at the gate, the light of day seemed of a darker colour than when I went in. I walked all the way to London, for I could not go back and see Drummle; I could not bear to sit on the coach and be spoken to.

It was past midnight when I crossed London Bridge. When I came to the gate of my house the night watchman gave me a note and told me that the messenger who had brought it begged me to read it before going to my rooms.

Much surprised by the request, I took the note. I opened it, the night watchman holding up his light, and read inside, in Wemmick's writing:

'Don't Go Home.'

Chapter 25   A Satisfactory Arrangement for Provis

I hired a carriage and drove to a hotel in Covent Garden where I spent the night. Early the next morning I went to see Wemmick in his house. He welcomed me and explained the mystery to me. He had heard, at Newgate prison, that they were looking for Provis and that my chambers in Garden Court were being watched and he had felt it necessary to give me warning. He had also found out that Compeyson was in London. He thought it safer for Provis to remain hidden in London for the time being, and not to attempt going abroad before the search stopped. Not finding me at home he had gone to Herbert at Clarriker's, and between them they had made satisfactory arrangements for the safety of Provis. They had housed him temporarily in the upper floor of the house down by the river where Clara, Herbert's young lady, and her old father, lived. This was a good plan, Wemmick told me, for three reasons. Firstly, this house was a long way from my chambers, and no one would look for me there. Secondly, without going near it myself, I could always hear of the safety of Provis through Herbert. Thirdly, whenever it might be safe to get him on board a foreign ship, there he would be, all ready, down by the river.

This made me feel very much happier, and I thanked Wemmick again and again. Then he advised me to keep in his house till dark, and left me to enjoy the company of his elderly father.

When it was quite dark I went out to find the place, which was called Mill Pond Bank. After losing my way several times, I came on it unexpectedly. I knocked at the door and an elderly woman of a pleasant appearance answered it. Soon Herbert came, and silently led me into the sitting room.

'All is well, Handel,' he said, 'and he is quite satisfied, though eager to see you. My dear girl is with her father (I heard him shouting upstairs); and if you'll wait till she comes down, I'll make you known to her, and then we'll go upstairs to Provis.'

As we were talking in a low tone, the door of the room opened, and a very pretty, slight, dark-eyed girl of twenty or so came in with a basket in her hand. Herbert gently took it from her, and presented her to me as Clara.

Provis lived in two rooms at the top. He expressed no alarm, and seemed to feel none. I told him how Wemmick had heard, in Newgate prison, that they were searching for him, and that my chambers had been watched; how Wemmick had recommended his keeping hidden for a time, and my keeping away from him. I added that when the time came for his going abroad, I should go with him, or should follow soon after him, as might be safest.

Then Herbert made a good suggestion. 'We are both good boatmen, Handel,' he said, 'and could take him down the river when the right time comes. Don't you think it might be a good thing if you began at once to keep a boat, and were in the habit of rowing up and down the river? You fall into that habit, and then who notices or minds?'

I liked this scheme, and so did Provis, and we agreed that it should be carried out. We also agreed that Provis should pull down the blind of his window with a view of the river whenever he saw us coming in our boat, as a signal that all was right. Then we wished him good night and left him.

When I had taken leave of the pretty, gentle, dark-eyed girl, and of the motherly woman in whose house she lived, I thought of Estella, and of our parting, and went home very sadly.

Next day I got the boat, and it was brought round to the Temple stairs, and lay where I could reach it within a minute or two. Then I began to go out for training and practice: sometimes alone, sometimes with Herbert. Nobody took much notice of me after I had been out a few times. At first I did not go far, but soon I began to go as far as Mill Pond Bank. Herbert saw Provis at least three times a week, and he never brought me any alarming news. Still I knew that there was cause for alarm, and I could not get rid of the idea of being watched. But there was nothing to be done, except to wait for a word from Wemmick.

Chapter 26   Estella's Mother

One day, I was taking a walk before dinner, when Mr Jaggers met me and invited me to eat with him in his house in Gerrard Street. I was going to excuse myself, when he added, 'Wemmick's coming.' I accepted, and we both went to his office, where he closed the business of the day, and then, accompanied by Wemmick, we took a carriage to Mr Jaggers's house.

As soon as we got there, dinner was served. My attention was attracted by his housekeeper, a woman of about forty, whom I had seen in Mr Jaggers's house on a previous visit. She was rather tall, extremely pale, with large faded eyes, and a quantity of streaming hair. On this occasion she was putting a dish on the table, at her master's elbow, when he addressed her, saying that she was slow. I observed a certain action of her fingers as she spoke to him. It was like the action of counting. She stood looking at him, not understanding whether she was free to go, or whether he had more to say to her. She looked at him very closely. Surely, I had seen exactly such eyes and such hands somewhere very recently!

He told her to go, and she left the room silently. But she remained before me, as plainly as if she were still there. I looked at those hands, I looked at those eyes, I looked at that flowing hair; and I compared them with other hands, other eyes, other hair, that I knew of, and with what those might be after 20 years of a cruel husband and a stormy life. And I felt absolutely certain that this woman was Estella's mother.

Dinner over, Wemmick and I took our leave early, and left together. On the way I asked Wemmick to tell me what he knew of her, and this is what he told me:

'About twenty years ago, that woman was tried for murder, but in the end they released her. She was a very good-looking young woman, but lived on the streets. Mr Jaggers defended her and handled the case in a quite amazing way. The murdered

91

person was a woman; a woman a good ten years older, and much stronger – also a street woman. It was a case of jealousy. Jaggers's client had been married very young to a small-time criminal. The murdered woman was found dead in a farm building. There had been a violent struggle, perhaps a fight. The murdered woman's skin was scratched and torn, and she had been held by the throat until her last breath.

'The accused woman had few marks on her, but the backs of her hands were scratched. Were these scratches caused by fingernails? Now, Mr Jaggers showed that she had struggled through a lot of sharp bushes; and it is true that the scratches could have been made by them. But the strongest point he made was this. She was strongly suspected of having, at about the time of the murder, killed her child by this man – some three years old – to revenge herself on him. Mr Jaggers claimed that if this were true – and there was no proof – then perhaps the scratches were made by the child and so the scratches were accounted for. But, as he said: "You are not trying her for the murder of her child." To sum up, Mr Jaggers was too clever for the jury, and they gave in.'

'Has she been in his service ever since?'

'Yes,' said Wemmick.

'Do you remember the sex of the child?' I asked.

'Said to have been a girl.'

We parted, and I went home, with new matter for my thoughts, though with no relief from the old.

◆

Miss Havisham had sent me a note, saying that she wanted to see me on a matter of business I had mentioned to her. So the next day I went to Satis House. The business referred to concerned Herbert. I had told her that I was trying to help a friend, but that I could not continue to do so, for reasons I was bound to keep secret. Now she asked me how much money was needed, and I said, 'Nine hundred pounds.'

'If I give you the money for this purpose, will your mind be more at rest?' she asked.

'Much more at rest.'

Then she wrote an order to Mr Jaggers to pay me the money. She was very sorry for the sadness she had caused me, and pressed my hand and cried desperately over it, 'Oh! What have I done? What have I done?'

'If you mean, Miss Havisham, what have you done to injure me, let me answer: very little. I should have loved her under any circumstances. Is she married?'

'Yes!'

It was a needless question, for a new emptiness in the house had told me so.

'If you knew all my story,' she said, 'you would have some pity on me and a better understanding of me.'

'Miss Havisham,' I answered, 'I do know your story, and I feel great pity for you. May I ask you a question about Estella's childhood? Whose child was Estella?'

She shook her head.

'You don't know?'

She shook her head.

'But Mr Jaggers brought her here, or sent her here?'

'Brought her here.'

'Might I ask her age then?'

'Two or three. She herself knows nothing, but that she was left without a father or mother and I adopted her.'

So convinced was I of that woman's being her mother, that I needed no evidence to establish the fact in my mind.

What more could I hope to do by extending the visit? I had succeeded on behalf of Herbert, and Miss Havisham had told me all she knew of Estella; so we parted.

Chapter 27   I Learn More of Provis's History

Herbert paid several visits to the house down the river where Clara, her father and Provis lived. One evening he said to me: 'I sat with Provis for two hours last night, Handel. He told me more of his life. He spoke about a woman he had had great trouble with. She was a young woman, and a jealous woman, and a revengeful woman; revengeful, Handel, to the last degree.'

'To what last degree?' I asked.

'Murder.'

'How did she murder? Whom did she murder?'

'Another and a stronger woman, in a farm building; there had been a struggle, and the other woman was killed. Mr Jaggers defended the murderer, and his success with that defence first made his name known to Provis.'

'Was the woman found guilty?'

'No; she was released. This young woman and Provis had a little child, of whom Provis was very fond. On the evening of the same night when the object of her jealousy was killed, the young woman presented herself before Provis and swore that she would destroy the child, and he would never see it again; then, she disappeared.'

'Did the woman do as she swore?'

'She did.'

'That is, he says she did.'

'Why, of course, my dear boy. He says it all. Now, the child's mother had shared four or five years of the awful life he described to us, and he seems to have felt pity for her. Therefore, fearing he would be called on to give witness about this murdered child and so be the cause of the mother's death, he hid himself, out of the way and out of the trial, and was only mentioned as a certain man called Abel, the subject of the jealousy. After the trial the mother disappeared, and thus he lost both her and the child. That evil man, Compeyson, knowing of his keeping out of the way at that time, and of his reasons for doing so, held the knowledge over his head as a means of keeping him poorer and working him harder.'

'Did he tell you when this happened?'

'About 20 years ago.'

'Herbert,' said I, 'look at me. Touch me. You are not afraid that I am feverish?'

'No, my dear boy,' said Herbert. 'You are rather excited, but you are quite yourself.'

'I know I am quite myself. And the man we have in hiding down by the river is Estella's father.'

Chapter 28   I Am Trapped

One Monday morning, when Herbert and I were at breakfast, I received the following letter from Wemmick:

Burn this as soon as read. Early in the week, or say Wednesday, you may do what you know of, if you want to try. Now burn.

◆

When I had shown this to Herbert and put it in the fire, we considered what to do.

'I have thought it over, again and again,' said Herbert, 'and I think I know a better course than taking a Thames boatman. Take Startop. He is a good fellow, a skilled man, fond of us, and very willing and quite honest. Will you go with Provis?'

'No doubt.'

'Where?'

It did not matter very much where we went, if only Provis was out of England. Any foreign ship that fell in our way and would take us would do. Our plan would be to get down the river on the day before such a ship was to leave London, and wait in some quiet spot until we could row out to it.

Herbert agreed, and we went out after breakfast to inquire about the times of the departure of ships, and found one for Hamburg that was likely to suit our purpose best. Startop was very willing to help us. He and Herbert would row, and I would guide the boat. Herbert was to prepare Provis to come down to the river bank on Wednesday, when he saw us approach, and not sooner.

These arrangements having been made, I went home. On opening the door of our chambers I found a letter in the box, directed to me. It said:

If you are not afraid to come to the marshes tonight or tomorrow night at nine, and to come to the little house by the lime kiln, you had better come. If you want information regarding Provis, you had better come and tell no one and lose no time. You must come alone.

I had had enough on my mind before this strange letter came. What to do now, I could not tell. I left a note for Herbert, telling him that I had decided to pay a short visit to Miss Havisham, and took the coach to the town.

It was dark before I got there. Avoiding the inn, I found a smaller place in the town and ordered some dinner. Having eaten it, I put on my coat and went out, heading straight for the marshes.

It was a dark and windy night; and the marshes were very unwelcoming. After a long walk, I saw a light in the little house near the lime kiln. I hurried to it and knocked at the door. There was no answer, and I knocked again. No answer still, and I tried the handle.

It turned and the door opened. Looking in, I saw a lighted

candle on a table, a bench and a bed. I called out, 'Is there any one here?' but no voice answered. I called again, but there being no answer I went out, not knowing what to do.

It was beginning to rain, so I turned back into the house, and stood just inside the doorway. Then, all of a sudden, the candle was put out and the next thing I knew was that someone had thrown a rope over my head and tied my hands to my sides.

'Now,' whispered a voice, 'I've got you!'

'What is this?' I cried, struggling. 'Who is it? Help, help!'

A strong man's hand was set against my mouth to silence my cries while I was tied tight to a ladder a few inches from the wall. 'And now,' said the voice, 'call out again, and I'll make short work of you.'

Then the man lit the candle, and I saw that it was Orlick.

'Now,' said he, when we had looked at one another for some time, 'I've got you.'

'Untie me. Let me go!'

'Ah!' he returned, 'I'll let you go. I'll let you go to the moon, I'll let you go to the stars. All in good time.'

He sat shaking his head at me, then he reached out and picked up a gun.

'Do you know this?' said he, pointing the gun at me. 'Do you know where you saw it before? Speak, dog!'

'Yes,' I answered. (I had seen it in his room in Satis House, when he was employed as gate keeper there.)

'You cost me that job. You did. Speak!'

'What else could I do?'

'You did that, and that would be enough, without more. How dared you come between me and a young woman I liked?'

'When did I?'

'When didn't you? It was you who always gave Old Orlick a bad name to her.'

'You gave it to yourself; you gained it for yourself. What

are you going to do to me?'

'I'm going to have your life. I won't have any piece of you left on earth. I'll burn your body until there's nothing left.'

He had been drinking, and his eyes were red. Around his neck was a tin bottle. He brought it to his lips and drank again.

'Dog,' said he, 'I'm going to tell you something. It was you that struck your sister down.'

'It was you,' said I.

'I tell you it was your doing. You were favoured, and Old Orlick was beaten and ignored; now you pay for it.'

He drank again, and became more violent. Then, taking up the candle, he brought it so close to me that I turned my face away to save it from the flame.

Suddenly he stopped, drank again, and bent down, and I saw in his hand a stone hammer with a long heavy handle.

Without one word of appeal to him, I shouted out and struggled with all my might. At the same moment I heard answering shouts, saw figures and a patch of light at the door, heard voices, and saw Orlick struggling with men. I saw him get away from them and fly out into the night.

Then I fainted. When I came to myself, I found that I was lying on the floor, in the same place, with my head on someone's knee, and another bending over me. It was Herbert and Startop. They bound my arm, which had been hurt in my struggle to free myself, with some cloth, and in a little while we were on our way back. Herbert told me how they had found me. I had, in my hurry, dropped the letter in our chambers, and Herbert, coming home with Startop, had found it soon after I was gone. Its tone made him anxious, the more so because it differed so much from the letter I had left for him. So he set off with Startop, and, with the help of a guide, they came to the little house near the lime kiln. Hearing my shouts, Herbert answered them and rushed in, followed by the other two.

Wednesday being so close upon us, we decided to go back to London that night. It was daylight when we arrived, and I went at once to bed and lay there all day. Herbert and Startop kept me very quiet, and kept my arm cleaned, and gave me cooling drinks. Whenever I fell asleep, I woke up suddenly, thinking the opportunity to save Provis was gone.

Chapter 29   Our Plan of Escape and How it Failed

Wednesday morning was one of those March days when the sun shines hot and the wind blows cold. We had our short sailors' overcoats with us, and I took a bag. Where I might go, what I might do, or when I might return, were questions completely unknown to me.

We went slowly down to the Temple stairs, and waited there, as if we had not quite decided to go on the water at all. Then we went on board and started, Herbert and Startop rowing, and I directing the boat.

Our plan was this. We intended to row down the river until dark. We should then be between Kent and Essex where the river is broad and lonely, and where the waterside residents are few, and where lonely inns are scattered here and there, of which we could choose one for a resting place. There we meant to hide, all night. The ship for Hamburg would start from London at about nine on Thursday morning. We would know at what time to expect it, according to where we were, and would call to it.

The cold air, the sunlight, the movement on the river freshened me with new hope. Old London Bridge was soon passed and now I, sitting in the back, could see the house where Provis was, and the landing stairs close by.

'Is he there?' said Herbert.

'Not yet,' I said. 'Yes, now I see him! Pull. Be careful,

Herbert. Slowly!'

We touched the stairs lightly for a single moment, and he was on board and we were off again. He had a cloak with him, and a black bag, and he looked as like a river pilot as my heart could have wished.

'Dear boy!' he said, putting his arm on my shoulder, as he took his seat. 'Faithful dear boy, well done. Thank you, thank you!'

He was the least worried of us all. It was not that he did not care, for he told me that he hoped to live to see me one of the best gentlemen in a foreign country; but he would not trouble himself about danger before it came upon him.

All day we rowed, except when we landed among some slippery stones to eat and drink. But night was falling fast, and I looked out for anything like a house.

At last we saw a light and a roof. We stopped, and pulled the boat out onto the bank for the night. We found the place to be an inn: a rather dirty place, but there was a good fire in the kitchen, and there were eggs and bacon to eat, and various kinds of drink. Also, there were two double rooms which we could have for the four of us. We had a very good meal by the kitchen fire, and then went up to bed.

I lay down with the greater part of my clothes on, and slept well for a few hours. When I awoke, I looked out of the window, and saw two men looking into our boat. They passed by under the window, and as it was still dark, I lost sight of them and fell asleep again. We were up early. I told the others what I had seen, and we agreed that Provis and I should walk away together to a certain point, and that the boat should pick us up there, in case we were being followed.

This plan was carried out, and when the boat passed us, we got in and rowed out into the track of the ship.

It was half past one before we saw her smoke, and soon after that, we saw behind it the smoke of another ship. As they were coming on at full speed, we got the two bags ready, and said goodbye to Herbert and Startop.

Then I saw another small boat shoot out from the bank only a little way ahead of us, and row out into the same track.

The ship was now very close. Soon the small boat crossed our path and fell alongside us. Besides the four rowers there were two men in it, one was an officer, and the other, who was wrapped up like Provis, seemed to cover his face, and whisper something to the officer as he looked at us.

Startop could make out, after a few minutes, which ship was first, and said to me, 'Hamburg' in a low voice. She was approaching us very fast, and the sound of her engines grew louder and louder. I felt as if her shadow were on us, when the men in the other boat called to us.

'You have a returned convict there,' said the officer. 'That's the man, wrapped in the cloak. His name is Abel Magwitch, otherwise Provis. I call on that man to give himself up; and you to assist.'

At the same moment he ran his boat into ours. The rowers were holding on to the side of our boat before we knew what they were doing. This caused great confusion on board the Hamburg ship; I heard them calling to us, and heard the order given to stop the engines, and heard them stop, but felt the ship driving down upon us. At the same moment, I saw the officer lay his hand on his prisoner's shoulder. Then I saw Provis jump and pull the cloak from the neck of the other man, and his face was that of the other convict of long ago. I saw him fall backward with a look of great fear, and I heard a great cry on board the ship and a loud splash in the water, and felt the boat sink from under me. Then I was taken on board the other boat. Herbert was there, and Startop was there; but our boat was gone, and the two convicts were gone.

Eventually a dark object was seen in the water. As it came nearer I saw it to be Provis, swimming. He was taken on board, and at once chained by the hands and feet. A careful look-out was kept for the other convict, but everybody knew he was drowned. They rowed towards the inn we had recently left, and here I was able to get some help for Provis, who had received a very severe injury in the chest and a deep cut on the head. He told me that he believed himself to have gone under the ship, and to have been struck on the head when rising. When he had laid his hand on Compeyson, Compeyson had stood up and fallen back, and they had both gone overboard together. There had been a struggle under water, but Provis had freed himself, struck out and swum away.

When I asked the officer for permission to change the prisoner's wet clothes by purchasing any I could get at the inn, he gave it readily, merely observing that he must take charge of everything the convict had about him. So the pocketbook, which had once been in my hands, passed into the officer's.

We remained at the inn until the tide turned, and then Provis was carried down to the boat and put on board. Herbert and Startop were to get to London by land, as soon as they could. I felt that my place was by Provis's side as long as he lived. For now my dislike of him had melted away, and in him I only saw a man who had meant to be my benefactor, and who had felt warm and grateful towards me. I only saw in him a much better man than I had been to Joe.

As we returned towards London I told him how sad I was to think he had come home for my sake.

'Dear boy,' he answered, 'I'm quite content to take my chance. I've seen my boy, and he can be a gentleman without me.'

No. I had thought about that. No. I knew that because he was a convict, his possessions would be taken by the government. But he need never know that his hopes of making me rich had come to nothing.

Chapter 30   Death of Provis

It was at this dark time of my life that Herbert returned home one evening and told me that he was leaving me soon. He was going to Cairo, on business. He asked me whether I had ever thought of my future, and when I told him I had not, he said:

'In our Cairo branch, Handel, we must have a . . .'

I saw that he did not like to say the right word, so I said, 'A clerk.'

'A clerk. And I hope it is not at all unlikely that he may become a partner. Now, Handel, will you come?'

I thanked him warmly, but said I could not yet be sure of joining him as he so kindly offered. He said that he would leave the question open for six months, or even a year, until I made up my mind. He was highly delighted when we shook hands on this arrangement, and said he could now take courage to tell me that he believed he must go away at the end of the week.

On the Saturday in that same week, I said goodbye to Herbert, who was full of bright hope, but sad and sorry to leave me, and then I went to my lonely home.

Provis lay in prison very ill, all the time he was waiting for his trial. He became slowly weaker and worse, from the day when the prison door closed upon him.

The trial came at last, and he was allowed to sit in a chair in the court, and I was allowed to stand close to him and hold his hand.

The trial was very short and very clear. Such things as could be said for him were said – how he had taken to working hard, and had made money lawfully and honestly. But the fact remained that he had returned to England. The punishment for his return was death, and he must prepare to die. I hoped and prayed he might die of his illness.

As the days went on, I saw a greater change in him than I had seen yet. 'Are you in much pain today?' I asked him one day.

'I don't complain of any, dear boy.'

'You never do complain.'

He had spoken his last words. He smiled, lifted my hand, and laid it on his breast.

'Dear Magwitch, I must tell you, now at last. You understand what I say?'

He pressed my hand gently.

'You had a child once, whom you loved and lost.'

A stronger pressure on my hand.

'She lived and found powerful friends. She is living now. She is a lady and very beautiful. And I love her!'

With a last faint effort he raised my hand to his lips; then his head dropped quietly on his breast.

Chapter 31   The Best of Friends

Now that I was left entirely to myself, I decided to give up the rooms I had shared with Herbert. I was in debt, had hardly any money, and I was falling very ill. For a day or two, I lay in my rooms, with a heavy head and aching body. Then, one morning, I tried to sit up in my bed, and found I could not do so.

I had a fever, and suffered greatly. I passed my days as though in a terrible dream. There seemed to be someone or other near me, and it seemed to be almost always Joe. At last, one day, I was able to ask, 'Is it Joe?' and his dear old voice answered, 'And so it is, dear Pip.' He had been with me all the time. News of my illness had reached him by letter, and Biddy had said, 'Go to him, without loss of time.'

Then he told me that I was to be talked to for only short periods, and that I was to take a little food at stated times, and submit myself to all his orders. So, I kissed his hand, and lay quiet, while he proceeded to write a note to Biddy, who, evidently, had taught him to write.

The next day he told me that Miss Havisham had died, that she had left most of her property to Estella, and four thousand pounds to Mr Matthew Pocket 'because of Pip's account of him'.

This piece of news gave me great joy, as it made perfect the only good thing I had done.

He also told me that Old Orlick had broken into Pumblechook's house, and had been caught, and put in prison.

As I became stronger, Joe became a little less easy with me, and addressed me with 'sir'. This hurt me deeply, but what could I say? Had I not given him reason to doubt my strong feelings for him, and to think that in my success I should grow cold to him and cast him off?

One morning I got up feeling much stronger. I went to his room, but he was not there, and his box was gone. I hurried then to the breakfast table, and on it found a letter. It said only this:

Not wishing to stay too long I have gone, for you are well again, dear Pip, and will do better without Joe.

P. S. Ever the best of friends.

With the letter was a receipt for my debt: Joe had paid it for me!

What remained for me now, but to follow him to the dear old forge, and show him how sorry and ashamed I was? I would go to Biddy, tell her how I lost all I had once hoped for, and remind her of our old confidences in my first unhappy time. Then I would say to her: 'Biddy, I think you once liked me very well. If you can like me half as well once more, if you can take me with all my faults and disappointments, I hope I am a little worthier of you than I was.'

In three days' time I was quite strong again. I took the coach to the town, and walked over to the forge. It was shut up and still. But the house was not deserted. The best sitting room seemed to be in use, for there were white curtains blowing at its window, and the window was open and bright with flowers. I went softly towards it, meaning to glance over the flowers, when Joe and Biddy stood before me, arm in arm.

I cried to see her, and she cried to see me; I, because she looked so fresh and pleasant; she, because I looked so worn and white.

'But, dear Biddy, how smart you are!'

'Yes, dear Pip.'

'And Joe, how smart *you* are!'

'Yes, dear old Pip, old chap.'

I looked at both of them, from one to the other, and then . . .

'It's my wedding day,' cried Biddy, in a burst of happiness, 'and I am married to Joe!'

They had taken me into the kitchen. They were both delighted and proud to see me, and delighted that I should have come by accident to make their day complete. I was glad I had not breathed a word to Joe about my hoping to marry Biddy. I congratulated them warmly, and thanked them again and again for all they had done for me. I told them that I was soon going abroad, and would never rest until I had repaid the money with which Joe had kept me out of prison.

'And now,' I said, 'though I know you have already done it in your kind hearts, tell me, both of you, that you forgive me.'

'Oh, dear old Pip, old chap,' said Joe. 'God knows I forgive you, if I have anything to forgive!'

'And God knows I do,' said Biddy.

Chapter 32   For Estella's Sake

I sold all I had, and paid what debts I owed, and went out and joined Herbert in Cairo. Many a year went round before I was a partner in the business; but I lived happily with Herbert and his wife, Clara, and wrote often to Joe and Biddy.

I had not seen them for 11 years when, one evening in December, I went once again to my old home by the forge. There, smoking his pipe in the old place by the kitchen fire, as healthy and as strong as ever, though a little grey, sat Joe; and there, in the corner, and sitting on my own little chair looking at the fire, was − I again!

'We gave him the name of Pip for your sake, dear old chap,' said Joe, delighted when I sat beside the child, 'and we hoped he might grow a little bit like you.'

In the evening I went out to look at Miss Havisham's old house, for Estella's sake. I had heard of her as leading a most unhappy life, that she had been separated from her husband, who had treated her with great cruelty and meanness; and I had heard of his death.

There was no house now, no brewery, no building whatever, only the wall of the old garden. The figure of a woman was moving towards me, and as I drew nearer I cried out:

'Estella!'

'I am greatly changed. I wonder you know me.'

The freshness of her beauty was indeed gone, but its indescribable loveliness remained.

We sat down on a bench that was near and I said, 'After so many years, it is strange that we should thus meet again, Estella, here where our first meeting was! Do you often come back?'

'No,' she said. Then, after a silence, she added: 'The ground belongs to me. It is the only possession I have not given up. Everything else has gone from me, little by little, but I have kept this.'

'It is to be built on?'

'At last it is. I have come to take leave of it before it changes. You live abroad still?'

'Yes.'

'And do well, I am sure?'

'Yes; I do well.'

'I have often thought of you,' said Estella.

'You have always held your place in my heart,' I answered.

'I little thought,' said Estella, 'that I should take leave of you in taking leave of this spot. I am very glad to so do.'

'Glad to part again, Estella? To me, parting is a painful thing. To me, the memory of our last parting has always been painful.'

'But you said to me,' returned Estella, '"God keep you, God forgive you!" And if you could say that to me then, you will surely say it to me now, when suffering has taught me to understand what your heart used to be. I have been bent and broken, but – I hope – into a better shape. Be as good to me as you were, and tell me we are friends.'

'We are friends,' said I, rising and bending over her, as she rose from the bench.

'And will continue friends even if we are far away from each other,' said Estella.

I took her hand in mine, and we went out of the ruined place, and as I looked across the fields in the calm evening light, I saw no shadow of another parting.

ACTIVITIES

Chapters 1-7

Before you read

1 Here are some of the characters you will meet in the first few chapters. Match the characters with what you think they say. Then check as you read.

   1 an escaped prisoner
   2 Mrs Joe Gargery, the unpleasant older sister of our young hero
   3 Miss Havisham, a strange, rich old woman
   4 Estella, a young girl who lives with Miss Havisham

   a 'Keep still, you little devil, or I'll cut your throat!'
   b 'Look at me. You are not afraid of a woman who has never seen the sun since you were born?'
   c 'With this boy? Why, he is a common labouring-boy!'
   d 'Where have you been, you young monkey?'

2 Find these words in your dictionary. They are all in the story.

   blacksmith   contempt   convict   forge   gin
   handcuffs   pantry   veil

Complete the following puzzle.

1. _ _ _ _ ▢ _ _ _ _
2. _ ▢ _ _ _
3. _ _ ▢ _ _ _ _ _
4. ▢ _ _ _
5. _ ▢ _
6. _ _ _ ▢ _ _ _ _ _ _
7. _ _ _ ▢ _ _

Clue for word down

Someone found guilty of a crime and sent to prison or given hard labour as a punishment

Clues for words across

   1 Their purpose is to hold a prisoner's wrists together
   2 A place where metal is heated and shaped into objects

3 If you feel this for someone, you do not respect them

4 A thin piece of material for covering a woman's face

5 Strong alcoholic drink

6 Someone who works with iron, making and repairing things

7 A room in a house where food is kept

3 Use your dictionary to check the meanings of these words.

brewery   dismissive   gravy   hulk   marsh   tar

Match the words with the correct meaning.

a in the nineteenth century, this was used as a prison ship

b an area of soft, low, wet land

c a black sticky substance used for making roads

d a place where beer is made

e a sauce made with meat juices

f refusing to take a person or idea seriously

After you read

4 Put these events in the order of the time at which they occurred.

..... **A** Soldiers catch two escaped convicts.

..... **B** Pip is chosen to visit Miss Havisham.

..... **C** Pip steals from his sister.

..... **D** Pip cries.

..... **E** Pip moves into his sister's home.

..... **F** Pip is made to drink Tar Water.

..... **G** One convict admits to a robbery.

..... **H** Pip and Estella play cards.

..... **I** Pip is beaten.

..... **J** Pip's convict fights a second convict.

..... **K** Pip is frightened by the arrival of the soldiers.

..... **L** Pip promises to help a convict.

5 Discuss the two convicts. What do you know about them? What do you think their relationship is?

6 What explanations can you give for the way in which Miss Havisham lives and the way in which she has brought up Estella?

Chapters 8–13

Before you read

7 This is the last sentence in Chapter 7. What do you think Pip wants in life?

'I walked home very unhappily, thinking about all I had seen, and deeply conscious that I was a common labouring-boy.'

8 Check the meanings of these words in your dictionary.

benefactor   cobweb   guardian

   a Which words are people?

   b Explain the difference between a *benefactor* and a *guardian*.

   c What creature makes a *cobweb*? What is its purpose?

After you read

9 Answer the questions.

   a Why does Pip lie about his experiences at Satis House?

   b How does Estella behave towards Pip on his second visit to the house?

   c Why are there also adult visitors at the house?

   d Why does Miss Havisham give money to Joe Gargery?

   e How does Pip feel about Estella?

   f What is the cause of Joe's fight with Orlick?

   g Why does Biddy come to live with the Gargerys?

   h How is Pip's relationship with Biddy different from his relationship with Estella?

   i What are Pip's 'Great Expectations'?

   j Who does Pip believe his benefactor is?

10 Imagine you are Pip. Describe what you see and feel when you go into Miss Havisham's room.

11 Describe Pip's feelings about Joe Gargery and about Biddy. Give reasons for your opinions. What do these feelings tell us about Pip's character?

12 Work with two other students. Act out the scene at the inn in which Mr Jaggers tells Pip and Joe his news.

Chapters 14–18

Before you read

13 How do you think Pip's life will change now? Will the change be for the better, do you think?

14 Find the word *lure* in your dictionary. Which two of the following words have a similar meaning?

persuade   deceive   support   encourage   abandon

After you read

15 Which of the characters in the story:

   a is Mr Jaggers's clerk?

   b is the 'pale young gentleman' from Satis House?

   c was abandoned on her wedding day?

   d wants to be a businessman?

   e shares rooms with Pip?

   f feels out of place in the city?

   g demands Pip's presence in the country?

   h admits to having no heart?

   i is now employed by Miss Havisham?

   j is in love with Clara?

   k allows Pip to kiss her?

16 Choose the word which best completes the sentences below.

impressed   respectable   uncomfortable   love
embarrassed   surprised   loses   common

   a Joe is very .... during his visit to Pip in London.

   b Pip is .... by the way Joe behaves.

   c Pip now thinks that Joe is very ....

   d Estella is .... by the way Pip has changed in London.

   e Miss Havisham wants Pip to .... Estella.

   f Orlick .... his job at Miss Havisham's because of Pip.

   g Herbert is not .... when Pip tells him of his love for Estella.

   h Estella stays with a .... family in Richmond.

17 What does Pip believe that Miss Havisham intends for him? Do you think that Pip is right about her intentions?

Chapters 19–22

Before you read

18 Make predictions based on the chapter headings.

We Fall into Debt

Who acquires debts?

How does this happen?

I Come of Age

Which birthday is Pip celebrating?

Estella and Miss Havisham Opposed

What do they argue about?

My Strange Visitor

Who is the visitor?

After you read

19 Explain the context of each of these remarks.

    a 'Then, Herbert, estimate!'

    b 'Never too soon, sir.'

    c 'So proud, so proud!'

    d 'Can the candle help it?'

    e 'It's death to come back.'

20 Discuss how Pip feels when he discovers the true identity of his benefactor, and how his plans are affected. How would you feel in his situation?

21 Work in pairs. Using your own words, act out Pip's first conversation with his benefactor after the latter's arrival at his rooms.

Chapters 23–27

Before you read

22 What do you think the relationship is between Pip's benefactor and the other convict he saw that night on the marshes?

After you read

23 Answer these questions.

    a What name is Abel Magwitch using now?

    b Why does he hate Compeyson?

   c What is the connection between Compeyson and Miss Havisham?

   d Who does Estella agree to marry?

   e Who does Pip think Mr Jaggers's housekeeper is?

   f How does Pip continue to help Herbert financially?

   g Does Miss Havisham know the identity of Estella's mother?

   h Who is Estella's father?

24 Explain how Herbert, Wemmick and Pip plan to get Provis out of the country and describe the arrangements they make. Would their plans be simpler or more complicated these days? If you wanted to help an escaped convict leave your country, what plans would you make?

Chapters 28–32

Before you read

25 How do you think the story will end for these characters?

   a Pip   **b** Estella   **c** Provis   **d** Joe   **e** Herbert

26 Find these words in your dictionary.

   cloak lime-kiln

   Group the following words with one of the above two words.

   coat wrap stone cover oven heat

After you read

27 In Chapter 28, Pip receives two letters.

   a Who are they from?

   b What do they say?

   c How does Pip respond to each of them?

   d How are lives changed as a result of his responses?

28 Do you think that Provis dies happy? Why/why not?

29 Explain what has happened to Estella since Pip last saw her.

30 How do you interpret the last sentence of the story? To what extent do you find this ending satisfying?

Writing

31 Describe Pip's character and how it is affected by his experiences.

32 Describe and explain any *two* of these relationships.

  1 Pip and Joe

  2 Pip and Provis

  3 Estella and Miss Havisham

  4 Joe and Mrs Gargery

  5 Pip and Orlick

  6 Provis and Compeyson

33 Imagine you are Pip. Write a letter to Joe, congratulating him on his recent marriage and apologizing for the way you have behaved in the past.

34 Write a letter from Provis to Pip, to be opened after Provis's death.

35 Imagine you are Estella. Write an account of your final visit to Satis House and your meeting with Pip. What memories did this meeting bring back for you?

36 Imagine that it is now five years after the end of the story. Write a chapter, from Pip's point of view, explaining what is happening to each of the surviving main characters and what has changed in their lives.

Answers for the activities in this book are available from your local
Pearson Education office or contact: Penguin Readers Marketing Department,
Pearson Education, Edinburgh Gate, Harlow, Essex, CM20 2JE.